The Massey Lectures Series

The Massey Lectures are co-sponsored by CBC Radio, House of Anansi Press, and Massey College in the University of Toronto. The series was created in honour of the Right Honourable Vincent Massey, former Governor General of Canada, and was inaugurated in 1961 to provide a forum on radio where major contemporary thinkers could address important issues of our time.

This book comprises the 2007 Massey Lectures, "The City of Words," broadcast in November 2007 as part of CBC Radio's *Ideas* series. The producer of the series was Philip Coulter; the executive producer was Bernie Lucht.

Alberto Manguel

Internationally acclaimed as an anthologist, translator, essayist, novelist, and editor, Alberto Manguel is the best-selling author of several award-winning books, including *A Dictionary of Imaginary Places* and *A History of Reading*. He was born in Buenos Aires; in 1982 moved to Toronto, Canada, where he became a Canadian citizen; and now lives in France, where he was named an Officer of the Order of Arts and Letters. He is the recipient of numerous awards and honours, including a Guggenheim Fellowship.

The City
of Words

Alberto Manguel

ANANSI

Published in 2007 by
House of Anansi Press Inc.
110 Spadina Avenue, Suite 801
Toronto, ON, M5V 2K4
Tel. 416-363-4343
Fax 416-363-1017
www.anansi.ca

Distributed in Canada by
HarperCollins Canada Ltd.
1995 Markham Road
Scarborough, ON, M1B 5M8
Toll free tel. 1-800-387-0117

11 10 09 08 07   1 2 3 4 5

LIBRARY AND ARCHIVES CANADA CATALOGUING IN PUBLICATION DATA

Manguel, Alberto, 1948–
The city of words / Alberto Manguel.

(CBC Massey lecture series)
Includes index.
ISBN 978-0-88784-763-9

1. Toleration. 2. Violence. 3. Literature and society.
4. Fiction — Social aspects. I. Title. II. Series.

HM1271.M356 2007   303.6   C2007-903437-3

Library of Congress Control Number: 2007928058

Cover design: Bill Douglas
Typesetting: Laura Brady, Brady Typesetting & Design

 **Canada Council
for the Arts** **Conseil des Arts
du Canada**   ONTARIO ARTS COUNCIL
CONSEIL DES ARTS DE L'ONTARIO

We acknowledge for their financial support of our publishing program the Canada Council for the Arts, the Ontario Arts Council, and the Government of Canada through the Book Publishing Industry Development Program (BPIDP).

Printed and bound in Canada

To Alice, Rachel, and Rupert,
to Nathan, Amanda, Naomi and Andrew —
who will no doubt find their own stories.

*"The love of liberty is the love of others;
the love of power is the love of ourselves."*

— William Hazlitt, *Political Essays*, 1819

Contents

INTRODUCTION:

WHY ARE WE TOGETHER?

"I will deal with each aspect of this question by fragments,
by unconnected pieces, because the passing from one area of
knowledge to another fans the pleasure and ardour of read-
ing. If I were to write the chapters of my book in a
continuous form, each time exhausting the chosen subject,
they would certainly be more complete, more comprehensive,
of a nobler character. But I fear lengthy texts, and you,
reader, are worthy and capable of grasping the whole by
means of a few random details, and of knowing the end by
learning the beginning."

— Jahiz, *The Book of Animals*, IX cen.

AFTER THE TWO World Wars of the past century, the exercise of assembling and disassembling countries gave birth
to two opposing impulses. One was to enlarge the notion
of society, to return to an altered version of the imperialistic model under the guise of a gathering of nations, none

primo inter pares, and to call this patchwork the Western
World or the Society of Arab Nations, the African Con-
federacy or the Pacific Rim Countries, the Southern Cone
or the European Union. The other was to reduce society
to a minimum common denominator, tribal if not famil-
ial, based on ancient ethnic or religious roots:
Transdnistria, the Basque Country, Quebec, the communities of Shiites or Sunnites, Kosovo. In both cases,
composite or singular, every society we conceive into
existence seeks its definition as much in a complex multi-
ple vision of itself as in its opposition to another. Every
border excludes as much as it includes, and these successive redefinitions of nation act like circles in the set theory
of numbers, overlapping and intersecting one another.
Caught between definitions of nationality and globaliza-
tion, between endemic loyalties and a chosen or enforced
exodus, the notion of identity, personal and social, has
become diffuse, uncertain. Within this endless flux, what
name do we assume, singly and in groups? How does
interaction with others define us and define our neighbours? What are the consequences, the threats, and the
responsibilities of living in a society? What happens to
the language we speak, supposed to allow us to communicate among us? In fact, why are we together?

When I mentioned to Ronald Wright, whose brilliant
Massey Lectures on the notion of progress were delivered
a few years ago, that a possible title for my talks might be
"Why are we together?" his response was: "What's the
alternative?" Of course there is no alternative. For better
or for worse, we are gregarious animals, condemned to or

blessed with the task of living together. My question does not imply that there is an alternative: instead, it seeks to know what some of the benefits and blights of togetherness might be, and how we manage to put this imagination of togetherness into words.

Less a question than a series of questions, less an argument than a string of observations, the subject of these lectures is a confession of bewilderment. I have discovered that, with the passing of the years, my ignorance in countless areas — anthropology, ethnology, sociology, economy, political science, and many others — has become increasingly perfected while, at the same time, a lifelong practice of haphazard readings has left me with a sort of commonplace book in whose pages I find my own thoughts put into the words of others. In the realm of storytelling I'm a little more at ease, and since stories, unlike scientific formulations, don't expect (reject, in fact) clear-cut answers, I can muddle around in this territory without feeling bullied into providing solutions or advice. Perhaps for this reason, these talks will have something unsatisfactory about them: because my questions must remain, in the end, questions. Why do we seek definitions of identity in words, and what is, in such a quest, the storyteller's role? How does language itself determine, limit, and enlarge our imagination of the world? How do the stories we tell help us perceive ourselves and others? Can such stories lend a whole society an identity, whether true or false? And to conclude, is it possible for stories to change us and the world we live in?
— ALBERTO MANGUEL, Mondion, 2007

I.

THE VOICE OF CASSANDRA

"Vain was the chief's and sage's pride
They had no Poet and they dyd!
In vain they schem'd, in vain they bled
They had no Poet and are dead!"
— Horace, *Odes IV:9* [trans. Alexander Pope, 1733]

LANGUAGE IS OUR common denominator.

Alfred Döblin, one of the greatest novelists of the twentieth century, was once asked in a questionnaire why he wrote: he answered that this was a question he refused to ask himself. "The finished book doesn't interest me," he said, only the book that is being written, "the book to come." Writing was for Döblin an action that sifted through our present into our future, a constant flow of language that allowed words to shape and name the reality which is always in the process of being formed. "Method has no place in art, folly is better," he wrote in a letter to the Italian poet T. F. Marinetti, after Marinetti had proposed, in the Paris *Figaro* of February 20, 1909, that artists adopt a "futurist method" to implement their craft, embracing "action, violence and industrial change." "Tend to your futurism," Döblin instructed his effusive colleague, "I'll tend my Döblinism." But what exactly was this "Döblinism"? Alfred Döblin had served as a medical officer in the German army during the First World War before setting up his practice in the slums of East Berlin, whose identity he portrayed in his most famous novel, *Berlin Alexanderplatz*, of 1929. He was a man of awkward contradictions: a Prussian Jew who late in life converted to Catholicism, a radical socialist who opposed the tenets of the Russian Revolution, a psychiatrist who admired Freud but doubted the dogmas of psychoanalysis, and a proponent of an exuberant literature that constantly contravened its own rules but who sought in the traditional books of the Bible the basic mythology of his fiction. His subject was the changing identity of the twentieth-century world, but his hero was the everyman Job of the Old Testament, suffering but not meek, vocal but not strident, the paragon of unjustified victimhood. In 1933, under threat by the rising Nazi regime, like so many other German intellectuals Döblin sought refuge in France with his family and, seven years later, after the occupation of Paris, escaped by a dangerous route through Spain and Portugal to the United States. There he was offered several jobs, including that of scriptwriter in Hollywood: several scenes from *Mrs. Miniver* are said to be by his hand. But Döblin felt terribly isolated in his exile, unable to find a shared language in the land of his hosts. When a fellow writer who had remained in Germany during the Nazi years accused those who had left of enjoying the "armchairs and easy chairs" of emigration, Döblin answered: "To flee from country to country — to lose everything you know, everything that has nourished you, always to be fleeing and to live for years as a beggar when you are still strong, but you live in exile — that's what my 'arm chair,' my 'easy chair' looked like." And yet, even in the isolation of exile, Döblin continued to be, in his own words, "possessed by the instinct to write."

After the war, from 1947 to 1956, Döblin wrote some of his most powerful books in which language itself, the abused German language, is, to a great degree, the protagonist: showing the gradual abuses of power in the Third Reich shaped through the gradual abuses of meaning in the Weimar Republic, in the saga *November 1918*; echoing the present evils of imperialism in the baroque vocabulary of the seventeenth-century, in *The Amazon Trilogy*; and even imagining a future society somewhat healed of its wounds by means of the critical language of psychoanalysis in *Hamlet or The Long Night Comes to No End*. Sadly, Döblin's work, with the exception perhaps of *Berlin Alexanderplatz*, has been largely and undeservedly forgotten. Nevertheless, his conception of language as an instrument both to shape and understand reality remains, I believe, utterly valid today. Language, for Döblin, is a living thing that does not "retell" our past but "represents" it: "it forces reality to manifest itself, it burrows into its depths and brings forth the fundamental situations, big and small, of the human condition." It lets us know, in fact, why we are together. Most of our human functions are singular: we don't require others to breathe, walk, eat, or sleep. But we require others to speak and to reflect back to us what we say. Language, Döblin declared, is a form of loving others.

Language, when it appeared in our distant prehistory, probably some fifty thousand years ago, as a conscious method of communication, demanded to be a shared instrument based on a common and conventional representation of the world that lent a group of men and women the conviction, however uncertain in its proof, that their points of reference were the same and that their utterings translated a similarly perceived reality.

This reality of the world conjured up through language was, paleontologists tell us, first presented to our consciousness as something magically material: in our beginning, words appeared to us as occupying not only time but also space, like water or clouds. The American psychologist Julian Jaynes argued that long after the development of language, when writing was invented some five thousand years ago, the deciphering of written signs produced in the human brain an aural perception of the text, so that the words read entered our consciousness as physical presences. According to Jaynes, "reading in the third millennium B.C. may therefore have been a matter of *hearing* the cuneiform, that is, hallucinating the speech from looking at its picture-symbols, rather than visual reading of syllables in our sense." Language, as we once knew, does not merely name but also brings reality into being: a conjuring act achieved by means of words, and by means of those accounts of reality's events that we call stories.

Stories, Döblin argued, are our way of recording our experience of the world, of ourselves, and of others. When Job in his suffering remembers the days in which the light of God still shone upon him, and declares that, in his goodness, "I was eyes to the blind and feet was I to the lame," the recounted memory is not enough: Job wishes to be able to put down his experience as a story, as testimony of his faith. "Oh, that my words were now written!" he says in his lament, "oh that they were printed in a book!" As Job, and as the author of Job, knew, stories distill our learning and lend it narrative form, so that through variations of tone and style and anecdote we can try not to forget what we have learned. Stories are our memory, libraries are the storerooms of that memory, and reading is the craft by means of which we can recreate that memory by reciting it and glossing it, by translating it back into our own experience, by allowing ourselves to build upon that which previous generations have seen fit to preserve. In the mid-eighteenth century, Rabbi Uri of Strelisk asked: "David was a gifted man, capable of composing psalms. And I? What can I do?" His answer was: "I can read them." Reading is a task of memory in which stories allow us to enjoy the past experience of others as if it were our own.

Under certain conditions, stories can assist us. Sometimes they can heal us, illuminate us, and show us the way. Above all, they can remind us of our condition,

break through the superficial appearance of things, and
make us aware of the underlying currents and depths.
Stories can feed our consciousness, which can lead to the
faculty of knowing if not *who* we are at least *that* we are,
an essential awareness that develops through confrontation with another's voice. If to be is to be perceived, as
that illustrious contemporary of Rabbi Uri, Bishop
Berkley, remarked (and in spite of all attempts to reduce
his observation to the absurd, it remains a daily experienced truth), then to *know* that we are requires knowledge
of the others whom we perceive and who perceive us.
Few methods are better suited for this task of mutual perception than storytelling.

Dreaming up stories, telling stories, putting stories into
writing, reading stories, are all complementary arts that
lend words to our sense of reality, and can serve as vicarious learning, as transmission of memory, as instruction
or as warning. In ancient Anglo-Saxon, the word for poet
was *maker*, a term that blends the meaning of weaving
words with that of building the material world. The definition has Biblical roots. According to the second chapter
of Genesis, after making Adam out of dust, God created
the fowl of the air and the beasts of the field, and brought
them to Adam to see what he would call them, "and
whatsoever Adam called every living creature, that was
the name thereof." This gift of naming is an ambiguous
one. Was Adam supposed to invent names for each creature, or was he supposed to know their names and to
pronounce them out loud, like a child calling out to a dog
or a bird for the first time? Later Talmudic commentators

blended both suppositions into one. They argued that Adam was the inventor of writing, and that by means of his craft he had made up the names that he had uttered, not according to his fancy but to the true nature of each creature, like poets who find the right words for that which they wish to describe. According to the Talmudic commentators, such was the power of God's gift of words that Adam not only lent animals confirmation of their being by naming them, but was also the first to name human societies as well. "God showed Adam the whole earth," reads an early Biblical gloss, "and Adam designated what places were to be settled later, and what places were to remain waste." To this ancient reflection, Döblin added this comment: "Adam is the sum total of human beings moving through time and unfolding within it." Adam's words, our words, allow us a place both in space and in time. "Sometimes," wrote the poet Eric Ormsby, "I have the feeling that words lead a private existence of their own, apart from us, and that when we speak or write, especially in moments of strong emotion, we do little more than hitch a ride on some obliging syllable or accommodating phrase."

Words not only grant us reality; they can also defend it for us. In the Middle Ages, Irish poets were supposed to be able to protect the fields of wheat and barley from vermin by "rhyming rats to death"; that is to say, by reciting verse over the fields in which the rodents had their nests. In the sixteenth century, Tulsi Das, the greatest of Hindi poets, author of a version of the *Ramayana* that includes the epic of Hanuman and his monkey army, the celebrated *Ramacaritamanasa* or *Holy Lake of the Acts of Rama,* was sentenced by the king to be locked up in a stone tower. Alone in his cell, Tulsi Das spoke his poem aloud and from the recitation rose the monkey hero Hanuman and his army who burst into the tower and freed their maker. In 1940, sixteen years after Kafka's death, Milena, the woman he had loved so dearly, was taken away by the Nazis and sent to a concentration camp. Suddenly life seemed to have become its reverse: not death, which is a conclusion, but a mad and meaningless state of brutal suffering, brought on through no discernable fault and serving no visible end. To attempt to survive this nightmare, a friend of Milena devised a method: she would resort to the books she had read long ago and unconsciously stored in her memory. Among the memorized texts was one by Maxim Gorki, "A Man Is Born." The story tells how the narrator, a young boy, strolling one day somewhere along the shores of the Black Sea, comes upon a peasant woman shrieking in pain. The woman is pregnant; she has fled the famine of her birthplace and now, terrified and alone, she is about to give birth. In spite of her protests, the boy assists her. He bathes the newborn child in the sea, makes a fire, and prepares some tea. At the end of the story, the boy and the new mother follow a group of other peasants: with one arm, the boy supports the mother; in the other, he carries the baby. Gorki's story became, for Milena's friend, a sanctuary, a small safe place into which she could retreat from the daily horror. It did not lend meaning to her plight, it didn't explain or justify it; it didn't even offer her hope for the future. It simply existed as a point of balance, reminding her of light at a time of dark catastrophe, helping her to survive. Such, I believe, is the power of stories.

Makers shape things into being, granting them their intrinsic identity. Still in a corner of their workshops and yet drifting with the currents of the rest of humanity, makers reflect back the world in its constant ruptures and changes, and mirror in themselves the unstable shapes of our societies, becoming what the Nicaraguan poet Rubén Darío called "celestial lightning rods" by asking over and over again "Who are we?" and by offering the ghost of an answer in the words of the question itself. This renders the maker a disturbing figure in a society that seeks, at all costs, stability and efficiency in order to achieve the highest possible economic benefit. Jorge Luis Borges, in an Swiftian utopia he imagined late in life, in 1970, when he had grown old and disappointed with the world, described the role of the maker in these terms:

"Another custom of the tribe are the poets. A man decides to line up six or seven riddling words. He cannot contain himself and shouts them out, standing in the middle of a circle formed by the witch-doctors and the common folk as they lie flat on the ground. If the poem does not excite them, nothing happens; but if the words of the poet move them, then they all draw away from him, silently, under a holy dread. They feel that he has been touched by the spirit; no one will speak to him or look upon him, not even his own mother. He is no longer a man but a god and anyone may kill him."

Döblin felt strongly this sense of being "condemned"

by literature to the state of pariah. In *Destiny's Journey*, the account of his flight and exile from Hitler's Germany, Döblin wrote of this alienating experience:

> I have been like a plant growing in the earth, have taken my nourishment here and there and remained as I was. I have never seriously examined what drove me to want this or that. I was driven, and I assumed without ceremony that it was I who was the driving force. I have never been concerned with what my *I* claimed to be, what it wanted or didn't want. Consciously, Socrates taught: Know thyself! But how can I know myself if I am simultaneously that which knows and that which is to be known? I have always looked about me, have observed and judged things critically and gathered experience, and when I lie down to die I will have protected myself from feelings that I consider to be weak. I have been active, moved among people for years, was a person like they were, a minor being, a microbe swirling in the waters with millions of others.

And here we must introduce a qualification or caveat to this craft that boasts of building reality out of words. It concerns two different methods or theories of defining a society and its identity, and consequently that of each of its citizens. One theory assumes that creative language and created reality are in fact separate epistemological entities, and that, while the former (poetry or storytelling) elaborates its system of knowledge through intuition and imaginative analogy, the latter (politics and its various branches, including economy and law) does so in an empirical fashion, and is therefore of greater practical and material value. The second theory holds that both entities (literature and politics) are inextricably intertwined, and that the invention of stories and the building of states depend mutually upon each other. Döblin was fully aware of this very ancient problem.

Aristotle, in the second book of the *Politics*, discussing the six types of political systems that he has imagined for six different castes of citizens, notes that these systems require a setting of symbolic value in which to develop; that is to say, a symbolic scaffolding upon which to build the city that will house them. The first man to realize this, says Aristotle, was the architect Hippodamus of Miletus, a contemporary of Pericles who, although he knew nothing of politics, was able to draw up the map of an ideal city-state. Hippodamus's city reflected the Greek demographical ideal: a limited number of citizens divided by the role they played within society. Patriarchal, since women had no ruling powers; democratic, in the sense that the affairs of the state were publicly debated; military but not expansionist, since the ideal state was by definition a limited space, designed for the happiness not of all humanity but of the select citizens whom the fates had caused to be born on this soil, and who were therefore justified in using slaves to work under them. To serve these metropolitan ideals, the city was divided into a number of different sections — merchants, magistrates, etc. — grouped around the central *agora*. Each section was in turn organized in a grid of squares or blocks of houses that is still the model of our cities today. Faced with this

pattern, an outsider could surmise the purpose of the city:
the establishment of a social entity limited unto itself, seg-
regationist and conservative, destined for a happy few. At
the beginning of our notion of nationality is the idea of
privilege.

The most famous of ancient ideal cities, Atlantis, exem-
plifies the same concept. According to Plato, the city of
Atlantis rose in the centre of a plateau, surrounded by
concentric rings of earthworks separated from one
another by deep canals. The central nucleus or first ring
was protected by a wide wall, and contained the seats of
power: the fortress, the Royal Palace, and the Temple of
Poseidon; in other words, the seats of the army, government, and religion. The first ring was separated from the
second one by a canal that served as an interior port,
allowing access to the military section: the second ring,
with the barracks, gymnasium, and racing-tracks, supple-
mented the requirements of the first. Another canal
separated the second from the third section, allotted to
the main port of Atlantis. Finally, one last canal divided
the port from the outer or fourth ring, which housed the
merchants' section. Plato's city is a physical mirror of the
social order, and for him, as for Hippodamus, the utopian
site must correspond exactly to the utopian ideal. In other
words, the city must be the reflection of the story told
about it.

But for Plato, while a symbolic or literary construction
must serve as the blueprint for the city, any literary imagination that does not lead to the concrete realization of a
perfectly run state has no place in his definition of society.

For that reason, the poets, the makers who construct not "the real thing" but phantoms that take the place of what is real, must be banished. Plato lends words to Socrates to explain this. Reason, Socrates says, constrains the philosopher to ban poetry from the ideal state. "We must know the truth," he admits somewhat reluctantly, because he loves the poetry of Homer, who must also be exiled from the well-governed Republic, "that we can admit no poetry into our city save only hymns to the gods and the praises of good men. For if you grant admission to the honeyed Muse in lyric or epic, pleasure and pain will be lords of your city instead of law and that which shall from time to time have approved itself to the general reason as the best." Laws and regulations, for the sake of efficiency, rule Plato's city, and poetry (literature in general) cannot have a place in it unless "it can be shown that she bestows not only pleasure but benefit." Plato (Plato's Socrates) seems to think that the reality created by words is noxious because it is not the wished-for reality, and that its imaginative creations, because they depict a mostly unflattering picture of who we and the gods are, should not be allowed in a city-state whose stories should be all cautionary or elevating. Most of the time, poets identify with the sins and errors of humankind, and ignore the higher qualities that must seem to their audience dull in comparison. And even when their poetry portrays the good and the virtuous, poets merely imitate these qualities without really attaining them. Most readers, Plato warns, remain on the surface of the text, delighting in the anger of Achilles or the cunning of Ulysses, enjoying the pain of Hecuba and the sacrifice of Iphigenia, without attempting to reach through these depictions a possible enlightenment. To the qualities of vicarious memory and knowledge implicit in stories, Plato (branding them as undesirable) adds those of vicarious happiness and of suffering, of goodness and of evil-doing. According to Plato, the identity granted by stories is as variable and arbitrary as that of a donned mask.

Plato is right, but not entirely. His audience, and that of the hundreds of generations of readers who succeeded him, have by and large sought in literature some form of, if not soothing entertainment, then at least of second-hand experience of the world, learning without action and fulfillment without accomplishment. Closer to our time, Carl Gustav Jung, in his incisive reading of the Book of Job, insisted that a deeper fulfillment and learning were possible through stories. According to Jung, in the Biblical story God runs the risk of allowing Job to be merely the Devil's victim, the passive actor of the world's sufferings. Job himself presents instead both sides of the question, as witness and as recipient of God's munificence and God's injustice. Only when God, as "reader" of the words Job wishes "were now written," is confronted with Job's recital, does the story come full circle: God the Maker learning through the experience of one of his creatures, through a man good enough to have been "eyes to the blind, and feet . . . to the lame." This, too, is Döblin's reading of the Book of Job: that, like the God of Job, every reader has this ultimately illuminating possibility. Not every reader, of course, profits from it: most readers prefer to remain safely this side of the page. But sometimes an epiphany occurs. "I read," noted Döblin, "like the flame reads the wood." This all-consuming reading that transforms reality is that of Rabbi Uri of Strelisk, who will build his own teachings upon the words of King David; of Tulsi Das, who will be rescued by his literary creations; of Milena's friend, who will find in Gorki's imagination the means to survive; of Alfred Döblin's readers, who will discover in his mirrors their own ever-shifting identity.

Döblin was fully aware that literary observation and critical judgement, however clearly expressed and imaginatively wrought, can never promise a revelation, and his best-known book, *Berlin Alexanderplatz*, never attempts to argue, only to convince by showing. *Berlin Alexanderplatz* is a vast, complex masterpiece that, much like Joyce's *Ulysses*, which was published seven years earlier, traces the currents and undercurrents of a city by following the peregrinations of one of its lesser inhabitants: in Döblin's case, the murderer Franz Biberkopf after his release from prison. Biberkopf is a far-from-innocent Job (whose book is quoted many times in the novel), subject to temptations and misfortunes, vaguely attracted to Nazi propaganda, and unattached to anybody or anything. "I did not conjure him up for the fun of it," Döblin wrote, "but to share his hard, true and illuminating existence." From that single existence it may be possible to construct a plural identity emerging from a geometrical progression of reflected others. "One is stronger than myself," Biberkopf says. "If there are two of us, it becomes even more difficult to be stronger than myself. If there are ten, it's more difficult still. And if there are a thousand, a million of us, then it becomes very, very difficult indeed!"

In 1945, Döblin returned from his American exile to Germany as a commissioned education officer, and over the next few years gave a series of talks in which he attempted to confront his defeated countrymen with the image of their shattered identity. For Döblin, the only way in which Germany could recover after Hitler was to find a collective identity that compounded personal freedom with a "pitiless objectivity." Speaking in Berlin in 1948, Döblin told his German audience: "You have to sit in the ruins for a long time and let them affect you, and feel the pain and the judgement." Reporting on Döblin's talk, the journalists complained that they had heard this kind of argument far too often, and that "it didn't help a bit that it came from a famous writer and infrequent guest." Döblin answered: "You haven't heard it. And if you heard it with your ears you didn't comprehend it, and you'll never comprehend it because you don't want to." As Döblin knew, in most cases the maker's role is that of the Cassandra, the Greek priestess to whom Apollo granted the gift of prophecy on condition that no one would believe her. Most makers suffer from Cassandra's curse: the readers' unwillingness to hear.

According to Homeric sources, Cassandra was the daughter of Priam and Hecuba. Later authors (Pindar and Aeschylus among them) tell us that when Cassandra and her brother Helenus were still infants, Hecuba forgot them in the temple of Apollo. Once the children fell asleep, Apollo's sacred serpents came and licked their ears: from then onwards, they possessed the gift of prophecy. Others say that Apollo himself gave Cassandra the gift against her promise of making love to him. She accepted, but after they had slept together, Apollo asked for one more kiss; when she turned her face toward him, he spat in her mouth, thereby ensuring that no one would believe her. During the siege of Troy, she warned the Trojans against the Wooden Horse of the Greeks and prophesized the fall of the city. Later, she became part of Agamemnon's booty and bore him twin sons. After Agamemnon was murdered by Aegisthus, the lover of his wife, Clytemnestra, Cassandra and her twins were killed by Clytemnestra herself.

Because Cassandra and her brother were forgotten by their mother, the myth has it, they were unlike the rest of Hecuba's children. In the language of the myth, as a consequence of this casual severing, Cassandra's individuality is thrust upon her in her infancy. She must learn to fend for herself and not rely on the teachings of her elders. The divine gifts she receives, good and bad, are her own, not those willed by her parents. Alone, she must define herself and her attachments, alone she must perceive those inside and beyond the walls of her city, alone she must imagine what "home" will be and what stories will take place in this "home" — all this not based on what she is told is hers but on what she chooses to identify as hers. Cassandra doesn't speak from received knowledge but from a unique imagination of reality that she then translates into narrative. Apollo's gift confirms this singularity: working from common words, Cassandra must conjure up her own vision of the world, which is not the one her fellow Trojans want to see. As Cassandra knows, her responsibility is not to convince but merely to say. "My silence cannot keep his body alive," she cries out in Aeschylus's *Oresteia*, when the Chorus reproaches her for announcing the murder of Agamemnon. "My Greek is clear but still no one believes it." To which the Chorus answers: "All oracles speak Greek and all darkly." The poet, the oracle, can only work with a shared language, but so keenly wrought that, at its best, it appears to its readers "dark," since it resists any summary clarification. This is the great richness and difficulty of literature: that it is not dogma. It states facts, but gives no definitive answers, declares no absolute postulates, demands no unarguable assumptions, offers no labelling identities. Cassandra's words, their depth of vision, their clarity of thought (because they are poetically true and cannot be uttered as simple slogans) are what brand her as a maker, and condemn her and her children to destruction.

As Döblin experienced in person, Plato's exclusion of all Cassandras, of all visionary poets, from the Republic, is a measure re-enacted by countless governments since: concretized in Hitler's Germany by the emblematic burning of "degenerate" books on May 10, 1933 that included those of Döblin. As a society, we know that the maker's essential function is to illuminate, to constantly induce us, the readers, to redefine our beliefs, enlarge our definitions, and question our answers, But at the same time, for fear of disruption and uncertainty, we attempt to relegate the maker's role to that of fabulist, equating fiction with lies and opposing art to political reality: spitting, as it were, into Cassandra's mouth.

Mocked, described as abnormal, consigned to death: that is the fate to which society condemns many of its true makers. Even those who are fêted, enshrined, and granted prizes and honours are, in most cases, destined to remain unheard. Before going to her death, Cassandra speaks to the Chorus, this time offering them not a fore-telling of their tragedy but the overwhelming, all-encompassing picture of her existence that, by exten-sion, is also ours:

> This was life
> The luckiest hours
> Like scribbles in chalk
> On a slate in a classroom.
> We stare
> And try to understand them.
> Then luck turns its back —
> And everything's wiped out.

Perhaps the task of every true maker-poet is to con-tinue scribbling on the slate after "everything's wiped out." The immortality demanded by the creator of any line that for unfathomable reasons stirs us, suggests that, outside our reader's will and within society's constraints, literature can build a reality more durable than flesh and stone, such as Cassandra's lament for the evanescence of life, or Döblin's troubled frescoes of society in the years preceding the Third Reich.

Destitute, exiled, bereft of his books and his friends, Döblin summed up in his journal his mission as a maker, as someone who through words attempted to reflect back to the reader the "original meaning" of things. Aware that, like Cassandra, his stories did nothing to prevent the catastrophe of history, Döblin found that his task was nevertheless not useless, merely incomplete:

> As I sit here now I discover that the catastrophe has not robbed me, it has revealed me. And that I profited from my poverty. One end result of 'original meaning': to it belongs justice. It is not only the natural world that is constructed purposefully, but also events, history. The true depth of history is inaccessible to us. And if at present there is no sign of justice — and justice is the only thing I possess in the aftermath of the catastrophe and the revelation of my poverty — then I have to recognize that this is not the only world.

Döblin goes on to say that the lack of justice in this world proves the existence of another reality. He is not, in spite of his conversion, talking of the fairy afterlife of theology nor of any metaphysical conceits. He is not referring to an ineffable state of being beyond the borders of our senses. He is speaking of a craft, the making of stories, from which, he says, "omens and coincidences and signs flow into the visible world." Döblin calls this movement "a sort of 'softening' of reality" that becomes, he says, "transparent" in the telling. Any label, any fixed or imposed identity that attempts to seal reality within the shroud of a dogma, can be dissolved through the inspired application of words.

This "transparency" of which Döblin speaks is a curious notion. Language, precisely because of its erratic ambiguity, attempts to convince us, its users, of its accuracy and weight by declaring itself an absolutist affirmation, a system of freezing the world into a state of fixed being. This is the law of the Baker, in Lewis Carroll's *The Hunting of the Snark*: "What I tell you three times is true." Of course, in spite of this popular assumption, every use of language proves the contrary: that language seizes reality not by turning it into stone but by reconstructing it imaginatively, by means of allusion, inference, and suggestion, through Döblin's "omens, coincidences and signs," as something permanently mobile, ultimately ungraspable: something "transparent." Language can therefore never serve the dictates of power, political, religious, or commercial, except as a catechism of fixed questions and answers because, in spite of its pretensions to precision, it can never affirm anything indefinitely. We "see through" the reality told by language, layer after layer, as in the cleansing of a palimpsest, so that our readings of stories become, in fact, endless, every story alluding to or suggesting another somewhere underneath it, none allowing itself to stand as the ultimate truth. In *Murder in the Dark*, Margaret Atwood says of this curious craft: "By the rules of the game, I must always lie. Now: do you believe me?"

This is the paradox. The language of politics, on the one hand, which purports to address real categories,

freezes identities into static definitions, segregates but
fails to individualize. The language of poetry and stories,
on the other hand, which acknowledges the impossibility
of naming accurately and definitively, groups us under a
common and fluid humanity while granting us, at the
same time, self-revelatory identities. In the first case, the
label bestowed on us by a passport and the conventional
image of who we are supposed to be under a certain flag
and within certain borders, as well as the blanketing eye
that we in turn cast upon people who appear to share a
certain tongue, a certain religion, a certain piece of land,
pin us all to a coloured map crossed by imaginary longi-
tudes and latitudes that we take to be the real world. In
the second, there are no labels, no borders, no finitudes.

"At this point in history," wrote Döblin in 1948, "people are obliged to organize themselves into nations, and
join other nations like themselves. But at the very
moment that this need is being realized, and that the
demarcation line between a third nation is drawn, this
need is mixed with the tendency to measure oneself
against a third and fourth nation and to dominate them
— though one knows, or should know, how little we are
masters of our own fate. And once again in the sea of history there comes a wave, but it merely crashes against the
mainland to be tossed back, surging, into the sea."

Döblin settled in Paris in 1951, disillusioned with his
fellow countrymen. Six years later, he returned to
Germany only to die in a nursing home in Baden-
Württemberg, but something in his writing suggests that
he may not have felt entirely defeated. Somewhere in the

multitudinous pages of *Berlin Alexanderplatz*, Franz Biberkopf has a casual encounter with an Eastern Jew who mysteriously seems to understand Biberkopf's search for a deeper, more wholesome identity, and who suggests to him that a form of healing might be achieved, in part at least, through stories. "The most important thing for a man are his feet and his eyes," this wandering Jew explains. "You must be able to see the world and go to it." Stories, according to Döblin, echoing Job's pathetic claim from better days, help the lame to walk and the blind to see.

To the limiting imagination of bureaucracies, to the restricted use of language in politics, stories can oppose an open, unlimited mirror-universe of words to help us perceive an image of ourselves together. In the realm of storytelling, as Plato realized, nothing is held to what the ideal city requires: the maker does not build to order and, though readings can be co-opted and poetry can become propaganda, stories continue to offer to its readers other imaginary cities whose ideals are likely to contradict or subvert those of the official Republic. Plato's concern seemed to be, not that Cassandra was cursed, but that the curse might not be effective and that, in spite of Apollo's deviousness, readers would still believe her words. Perhaps, as Döblin knew, this cautious faith lies at the heart of every maker's craft.

II.

THE TABLETS OF
GILGAMESH

*"Do you know, I always thought Unicorns were fabulous
monsters, too? I never saw one alive before!"*

*"Well, now that we have seen each other," said the
Unicorn, "if you'll believe in me, I'll believe in you. Is
that a bargain?"*

— Lewis Carroll, *Alice's Adventures
Through the Looking-Glass*

ONE AFTERNOON late in 1872, in a dusty room of the
British Museum, a young curator who had been studying
a number of cuneiform tablets shipped back by an ama-
teur archaeologist from the recently uncovered ruins of
King Ashurbanipal's library in Nineveh, suddenly began
to tear off his clothes and dance around the tables in an
ecstasy of joy, to the restrained astonishment of his colleagues. The name of the excitable curator was George
Smith and the reason for his excitement was that he had

suddenly realized that he was reading "a portion at least of the Chaldean account of the Deluge." Spurred on by the find, Smith then began to look for other fragments of the account among the thousands of similar tablets and eventually, after "long and heavy work," was able to piece together a Mesopotamian version of the story of Noah's Flood, which he presented at the meeting of the Society for Biblical Archaeology on December 3, 1872. Smith thought that he had uncovered proof (if proof was necessary) of the Bible's truth.

We know today that the Nineveh tablets, written in an Akkadian dialect from the second millennium B.C., contain a single long poem penned or revised by a scholar-priest called Sin-leqi-unninni, who probably collated a number of older Akkadian texts, themselves based on ancient Sumerian originals. Like Homer, Sin-leqi-unninni may have truly existed or he may have been a literary invention, an author created by later readers to justify a colossal poem. Whichever the case, his poem, the *Epic of Gilgamesh*, is one of the oldest and most powerful stories we remember.

The *Epic of Gilgamesh* is the story of both a man and of a city, of how a man, King Gilgamesh, came to know who he was, and of how a city, Uruk, became not only magnificent but just. The epic starts with an exhortation to the reader, handing over to us, across the many centuries, the responsibility of learning. You and I, the poet tells us, must enter the city of Uruk and seek in its foundations a copper box containing the lapis-lazuli tablets on which the story of Gilgamesh is written. This, as far as we know, is the earliest "book-within-a-book" device in the history of literature. Here all stories begin.

Gilgamesh is the strongest of men, "huge, handsome, radiant, perfect," two-thirds divine and one-third human. But Gilgamesh is also a tyrant who abuses his authority, oppressing the men and raping the women. Unable to bear his injustice any longer, the people of Uruk call up to Heaven for reparation. The gods hear their complaint and understand that for Gilgamesh to become just, he requires a counterpart, someone who will balance the abuse of royal power so that peace will return to the city. They create Enkidu, the wild man who, as the mirror-image of Gilgamesh, is two-thirds animal and one-third human. Strong but gentle, living among the beasts whom he also protects, Enkidu has no knowledge of his own humanity and natural sense of justice. One day, a young trapper discovers Enkidu in the forest. Terrified, he tells his father that he has seen a savage creature who eats grass and drinks from the waterhole, and frees the animals from the trapper's snares so that he can catch nothing. "Go to Uruk," his father says, "go to Gilgamesh, / tell him what happened, / then follow his advice. He will know what to do." Gilgamesh orders the trapper to seek out the priestess Shamhat and to take her into the forest. There she is to strip naked and lie with her legs apart until Enkidu approaches. Enticed by Shamhat's charms, Enkidu will surrender. The trapper obeys and the priestess does as she is told. The *Epic of Gilgamesh* contains our first account of Beauty and the Beast.

Everything comes to pass as Gilgamesh has foreseen.

Enkidu and Shamhat make love for seven days. Afterwards, the animals shy away from him. Having gained
the beginning of self-awareness, Enkidu has lost his animal innocence. He now knows that he is human, and the
animals know it too. Dressed in one of Shamhat's robes,
his hair cut, his body washed and oiled, he is taken into
the city to confront Gilgamesh.

In the meantime, Gilgamesh has a dream: a star shoots
across the morning sky and falls before him like a huge
boulder. He tries to lift it, but it is too heavy, so he
embraces and caresses it. There the dream ends. Gilgamesh's mother explains: the boulder is a dear friend, a
mighty hero, whom Gilgamesh will take in his arms and
caress "the way a man caresses his wife." "He will be
your double, your second self," she tells him. "May the
dream come true," Gilgamesh answers. These words are
important, signalling that something in Gilgamesh, some
unconscious stirring in his mind, desires the union with
the other.

Enkidu challenges Gilgamesh, and the two strong men
fight, "limbs intertwined, each huge body / straining to
break free from the other's embrace." At last, Gilgamesh
succeeds in overthrowing Enkidu and pinning him on the
ground. Then Gilgamesh fulfills his dream. He takes
Enkidu in his arms and the two men embrace and kiss.
"They held hands like brothers. / They walked side by side.
They became true friends." Their adventures begin. Now
that they are two, the friends can face all dangers that
threaten the city-state: among them, a fierce monster called
Humbaba, a creature from outside both the civilized circle

of Gilgamesh and the natural circle of Enkidu, a demon who, deep inside the forest, attacks the people of Uruk on their travels. To vanquish Humbaba, Gilgamesh and Enkidu support each other and calm each other's fears. Fear bred from civilization is tempered by the knowledge of the natural world and vice versa, each man drawing strength from his own experience and intuition.

After the killing of the monster, the goddess Ishtar falls in love with Gilgamesh, but he rejects her. As a punishment, she begs her father, the god Anu, to send down the Bull of Heaven to kill the two friends. The god complies with his daughter's wishes, but Gilgamesh and Enkidu prove to be stronger than the beast and kill it. Unfairly (because there is as little justice in heaven then as now), the gods decide that by killing the bull, the friends have insulted them and that one of the two heroes must die. Enkidu is chosen as the victim. But Gilgamesh will not resign himself to the loss of his beloved and, moaning "like a dove," as the poem says, descends into the Underworld in an attempt to bring him back to life. Here he speaks to the souls of the departed and is told from the lips of a Mesopotamian Noah the story of the Flood (this is the fragment first deciphered by George Smith.) But now, deprived of his companion, Gilgamesh can no longer accomplish fabulous deeds. Empty-handed, he returns to his city.

And yet, this return is not a defeat. In the sequence of magical events that make up the epic adventure, Gilgamesh has acquired a deep knowledge of the meaning of death: not only that it is our unavoidable common lot,

but that its communality extends to life itself; that our life
is never individual, but that it is endlessly enriched by the
presence of the other, and consequently impoverished by
his absence. Alone, we have no name and no face, no one
to call out to us and no reflection in which to recognize
our features. It is only after Enkidu has died that Gilgamesh realizes the extent to which his friend is part of
his own identity. "O Enkidu," Gilgamesh weeps, "you
were the axe at my side / in which my arm trusted, the
knife in my sheath, / the shield I carried, my glorious
robe, / the wide belt around my loins, and now / a harsh
fate has torn you from me, forever." If the *Epic of Gilgamesh* carries a teaching, it is that the other makes our
existence possible.

A double bind illuminates and enlarges the reflected
protagonists, Gilgamesh and Enkidu, who are, so to
speak, the prototype, since the history of literature can be
read as the history of such bindings. Amorous couples,
couples of friends, of colleagues, of enemies, of master
and servant, of teacher and pupil: the combinations are
many and never exclusively of one kind. Adam and Eve,
Eros and Psyche, Electra and Clytemnestra, Job and Jeho-
vah, Cain and Abel, Dr. Faust and Mephistopheles,
Macbeth and Lady Macbeth or Macbeth and Banquo,
Sherlock Holmes and Watson, Kim and the Lama, Bou-
vard and Pécuchet — an infinity of characters oppose,
complement, instruct, and struggle against each other on
the pages of our books.

In Europe, in the eighteenth and nineteenth centuries,
the fear instilled by the growing mechanization of human

activities — fear that our humanity would be replaced by an evil simulacrum — gave birth to the notion of the other as the tangible presence of a hidden self: the other seen not as foreign, not as someone else from whom we can distance our own identity, nor as a flattering reflection of an idealized self-portrait, but as the secret, ultimately unknowable interior, the dark side of the heart. The other became the Doppelgänger or double: he had the features of the protagonist but preserved his opposite identity, as if that of a shadow being. In Germany, E. T. A. Hoffman was one of the earliest to develop the theme of the double in several of his fantastic fictions. His first novel, *The Devil's Elixir*, of 1815, is the story of two brothers, one a monk and the other a count, who resemble each other so greatly that the count, after an accident, believes that he himself is his own brother, living the other's life and thinking the other's thoughts. "I am the action of your thoughts," says an apparition in Heinrich Heine's long poem *Germany: A Winter's Tale*, which Heine wrote in 1844. Five years earlier, Edgar Allan Poe published a story, "William Wilson," in which both action and thoughts diverge and then coalesce: the protagonist begins as one, splits into two, and is unified once again in the end, when the double, ("my antagonist" Poe calls him) like the image in a mirror, says to the self who has just killed him: *"You have conquered, and I yield. Yet henceforward you are dead — dead to the World, to Heaven and to Hope! In me didst thou exist — and in my death, see by this image, which is thine own, how utterly thou hast murdered thyself."* This final, terrible lesson must be ours. The

other, through whose presence we become aware of our
own being, is transformed by us into our enemy at
the cost of our life, since whatever we do to him we
do to ourselves. This is the lesson of Gilgamesh, for
whom Enkidu's death must be mourned by the whole
world, since he was part of the world as he was part of
Gilgamesh:

> May the paths that led you to the Cedar Forest
> mourn you constantly, day and night,
> may the elders of great-walled Uruk mourn you,
> who gave us their blessing when we departed,
> may the hills mourn you and the mountains we climbed,
> may the pastures mourn you as their own son.

The nature of the double (to give the other its literary
name) is ambiguous, someone identical to and yet unlike
us, the image in a mirror in which left is right and right is
left. The double is human and yet not entirely so; of flesh
and blood but with an element of unreality because we
fail to recognize or identify every one of his actions. For
Gilgamesh, the double is Enkidu civilized into friendship,
but he is also Enkidu the wild man, familiar with the
woods and rocks. He is our neighbour, our equal, but also
the foreigner, the one who does things differently, has a
different colour, or speaks a different language. To better
differentiate us from him, we exaggerate his superficial
characteristics.

The first doubles were merely monstrous: other men
and women whom nature had granted different attributes

from ours. They were bigger, smaller, of other colours, with animal features, they flew or had only one leg or devoured one another's flesh. Ulysses met some on his travels (gigantic cannibals such as the Cyclops or the Laestrygonians, or birdlike women such as the Sirens) but even outside fiction they were carefully accounted for. The naturalist Pliny the Elder, writing in the first century A.D. and basing his accounts on much earlier chronicles, attributed to real people fantastical characteristics, a quality he *a priori* dismissed: "Among these [people] are some that I do not doubt will appear fantastic and unbelievable to many. For who believed in the Ethiopians before seeing them?" Pliny then lists a number of wonderful folk: the Arismaspi, "noted for having one eye in the middle of the forehead" and for battling with griffins; the inhabitants of Abarimon "who have their feet turned back behind their legs [and] run with extraordinary speed"; the Albanians, who are "bald from childhood and see more at night than during the day"; the Ophiogenes, who "cure snake-bites by touch"; the Psylli, who "produce in their bodies a poison deadly to snakes"; the Gymnosophists, who "remain standing from sunrise to sunset in the burning sun . . . resting first on one foot and then on the other"; the Monocoli, "who have only one leg and hop with amazing speed" and who, when the weather is hot, "lie on their backs stretched out on the ground and protect themselves by the shade of their feet"; the Machyles, "who are bisexual and assume the role of either sex" in turn.

Among the strangest of the people listed by Pliny are

the Cynocephali or Dogmen, whose heads are like that of dogs and whose bodies are covered with wild beasts' skins. "They bark instead of speaking and live by hunting and fowling, for which they use their nails." These Dogmen (and many other of Pliny's strange folk) appear in a later chronicle of the adventures of Alexander the Great in India, a medieval best-seller known as the *Alexander Romance*, attributed to a nephew of Aristotle called Callisthenes who accompanied Alexander on his excursions. The first versions of the book date from before the fourth century A.D., but it was succeeded by revised and improved translations in Latin, Armenian, Arabic, Pahlevi, Syriac, and Ethiopic. The American scholar David Gordon White noted that, with the addition of new material, "the specific names of Alexander's monstrous enemies was revised to fit current events," so that the "monstrous other" would be brought up to date with each new edition. In this way, the Dogmen of the *Alexander Romance* would come to be identified, according to the various versions, with the Scythians, the Parthians, the Huns, the Alans, the Arabs, the Turks, the Mongols, and a host of other real or imagined races. This is how the *Alexander Romance*, in several of its versions, describes Alexander's encounter with the Dogmen:

> We came to a place where a delightful and abundant spring rose . . . Then there appeared to us, about nine or ten o'clock, a man as hairy as a goat. . . . I was startled and disturbed to see such a beast. I thought of capturing the man, for he was ferociously and brazenly barking at us. So I

ordered a woman to undress and go to him on the chance that he might be vanquished by lust. But he took the woman far away with him, and, sad to relate, he ate her up.

Alexander's woman seems to have had less luck than Gilgamesh's priestess, but the tactics for domesticating the wild man are notably the same in both stories.

In the Judeo-Christian tradition, the Dogmen belong to the races excluded not only from Eden but from the "civilized" earth restored after the Flood. They are nevertheless human. Ham, Noah's son who dared to look upon his father's nakedness (and who, as a punishment, begat the black Ethiopians) is supposed to have had a son, Nimrod the Hunter, builder of Babel and the ancestor of the Dogmen. According to Saint Augustine, this monstrous race must be considered, like ourselves, children of God since "anyone who is born anywhere as a man — that is, a rational and mortal being — derives from that one first-created human being [i. e., Adam]. And this is true, however extraordinary such a creature may appear to our senses in bodily shape, in colour, or motion, or utterance, or in any natural endowment, or part, or quality." The Dogmen were blessed with the head of a familiar and loyal creature; perhaps a man with the head of another beast might have been more difficult to embrace. A man with the head of a dog, however, had something reassuringly domestic about it.

If the Dogmen, as Augustine suggested, were indeed human, and therefore candidates for redemption in the Second Coming, then they could also follow the teachings of Christ in our time. In the fifth-century Ethiopic book of saints, *Contendings of the Apostles*, the story is told of how Saint Andrew and Saint Bartholomew, travelling among the Parthians, meet a Dogman, a flesh-eating inhabitant of the City of Cannibals (Cannibal deriving from the Latin *cane*, dog). An angel has told the Dogman that, if he follows the two apostles, God will save him from the fires of hell to which his actions have condemned him. The Dogman accepts the angel's words and presents himself to the two saints. "He was four cubits in height and his face was like unto that of a great dog, and his eyes were like unto lamps of fire which burned brightly, and his teeth were like unto the tusks of a wild boar, or the teeth of a lion, and the nails of his hands were like unto the claws of a lion, and his hair had come down over his arms to look like the mane of a lion, and his whole appearance was awful and terrifying." The Dogman, whose name is Abominable, is thereafter given the name of Christian. Later on, Christian becomes transformed into Christopher, the giant saint who carries the Child Jesus across the river, after which the savage pagan is baptized by Saint Babylus at Antioch and changes, like Enkidu, into a civilized white man. Saint Christopher, as the carrier of Christ, was probably associated with the ancient Egyptian god Anubis, the dog-headed divinity who helps the souls of the dead cross into the Afterlife.

Muslim tradition attributes the Dogmen decadency not to Ham and Nimrod but to Noah's son Japhet, who, after the death of his wife, had his son suckled by a bitch, thereby giving the boy doglike features. His descendants are the people Alexander encountered in what is today Croatia, and are supposed to be brave fighters, always on the side of justice. Dogmen are also mentioned in the Indian and Chinese traditions. In the former, the dog is considered the last subhuman incarnation. A cult of Shiva, dating from the thirteenth century, calls for its devotees to behave like howling and barking Dogmen. In China, a number of medieval chronicles speak of the Dogmen whose kingdom lies beyond the limits of the Chinese empire and who are descended from the union of humans with dogs or wolves. One of the tasks of these Chinese Dogmen is to help lost travellers find their way back home, and protect them from wild beasts and highwaymen.

The notion of the other as both terrible and helpful is established early on in our history. According to a Talmudic reading of Genesis, after Cain is expelled from Eden for having killed his brother, God gives him a dog as protection from the wild beasts, and also to mark him as a sinner. These two functions grant the dog the double qualities of pariah and protector, but don't lend the dog a moral quality that only humans can possess. When the nature of the dog becomes part of that of the human being and the race of Dogmen appears, it acquires a similar amoral, not immoral, quality. The Dogman's actions are not faulty: they are merely outside the moral realm. In the eyes of any given society, this is a useful quality for a foreigner to have, since he can then serve the citizens by doing deeds that, in a member of that society, would be considered contrary to morals and therefore forbidden. (Accordingly, Orthodox Jews employ Gentiles as helpers on the Sabbath when they are forbidden to do any work, to switch on the lights or turn on appliances.)

In the *Epic of Gilgamesh,* this incorporation of the exotic into the familiar happens without reference to the political circumstances within which the story takes place. In later tellings, however, these circumstances become pivotal, and the story of the conflict between what is outside and what inside acquires specific historical features. So prevalent is this theme that literature can be read as a continuous chronicle of the resolution and restatement of a defining opposition, since every time a new identity is created, a new exclusion to that identity is simultaneously defined. Every homebred Gilgamesh requires its exotic Enkidu.

The word *exotic* comes from the Greek, *exotikos,* meaning "outside," that is to say, that which is not contained within the city's walls. For centuries, in the eyes of Europeans, the idea of home, of what lies "inside," coincided with the idea of the West. "Outside" was all the rest: the unfamiliar, the uncanny, the exotic Orient that lay beyond the horizon. "Outside" was for the medieval Europeans bits of Africa and of Asia: the dark skins and precious ivory of Ethiopia, the opulence of India, the rituals of China, the mysteries of Japan, the secret cultures of Burma and Korea, the luxurious and brutal Russian Empire, the vast deserts of unexplored Mongolia. From the Orient came everything foreign, that is to say, everything strange and forbiddingly sensuous, what St. Bernard called "the temptation of the exotic." Also, the fear of the unknown, the fear of those Barbarian invaders whose cultures threatened the perceived supremacy of Occidental culture as a menace to the kingdom of Christ. Marco Polo's tall tales and Sir Thomas Mandeville's imaginary journeys were literary incursions to claim from the "exotic" regions if not allegiance with, then submission to, the West, harping on the accounts of their differences. The Crusades were the punitive advances of landlords who wanted to claim what they perceived as the usurped properties of Christendom, but they were also attempts to wall in the strange "outside" of the Orient, to domesticate the exotic. The Arab amazement at the brutality and senselessness of these crusading invaders stems in part from the reflection in a mirror: the self suddenly perceived as an exotic other, who becomes in turn another perceiving self.

As opposing symbols of this distinction, the West proposed "the Cross of Christ" triumphing over "the Labyrinth of the Heathen" (according to Saint Augustine), a dichotomy to which later Arab commentators responded with the "Holy Qumran of the Believers" crushing "the crossed sticks" that make up "the Sign of the Infidels." The term *infidel* is, for Muslims, the ultimate "exotic" term meaning "he who lies utterly outside the realm of God's people," and was applied to the invaders from the West as early as 1158 by the historian Ibn al-Qalanisi, who added to the insult the redundant curse "May God forsake them." The Europeans (the people from the West) became known at the time of the Crusades as *Ifranj* or *Firanj*, probably meaning "a subject of Charlemagne's empire," which gave rise to such denigrating

words as *tafanaja* ("to become Europeanised") and *al-ifraji*
("syphilis"), the exotic malady *par excellence*.

The image of the West as a land of mortal danger for a
Muslim casts a long shadow. In March 2007, the major
Saudi newspaper, *Al-Watan*, reported that young Saudis
wishing to study in the West with a government grant
had to undergo an obligatory preparatory course in
which they were warned against the dangers awaiting
them in non-Islamic lands. Among other cautions, they
were advised, when having to lodge in non-Muslim
households, to "stay away from families with daughters,"
"not to remain on their own with the mother," and, if they
decided to marry a foreigner, to be aware that, according
to Islamic law, they would be forced eventually to
divorce, "though they were not obliged to inform their
would-be spouses of this fact." "Such absurd arguments,"
says *Al-Watan*, "stem from the conventional attitude of
demonizing the other. To divide the world in 'Muslim'
and 'non-Muslim' territories is in open contradiction with
the reality of the modern world in which different popu-
lations mingle."

The novelist Oliver Goldsmith, writing in 1760,
observed: "Should it be alleged in defense of national
prejudice, that it is the natural and necessary growth of
love to our country, and that therefore the former cannot
be destroyed without hurting the latter, I answer, that this
is a gross fallacy and delusion. That it is the growth of
love to our country, I will allow; but that it is the natural
and necessary growth of it, I absolutely deny. Superstition
and enthusiasm too are the growth of religion; but who

ever took it in his head to affirm that they are the necessary growth of this noble principle?"

Perhaps this is one of the reasons why we are together, why Gilgamesh and Enkidu once sought each other out in a land that seems today destined to anything but togetherness, a land relentlessly drifting into a patchwork of opposing families and tribes, a land in which Enkidu repeatedly dies and Gilgamesh continues to mourn, forgetting that once upon a time they stood side by side in their adventures.

Enkidu's death and Gilgamesh's lament are not, however, the final moments of the poem. Framing their adventures, at the beginning and at the end, is a eulogy of Uruk, "which no city on earth can equal," causing the reader to wonder: In what way do the deeds of its heroes (the king inside its walls and the wild man outside them) help understand the character of the imperial metropolis? How does the epic of a coming-together of artificial civilization and the natural world become the history of the city state itself? It is as if, for the Akkadian author of the epic, Enkidu's sacrifice and Gilgamesh's sorrow were required for the city's greater glory, as if the adventures of the two friends increased in some mysterious way Uruk's power and prestige, granting it in the process a heroic identity, that of a double in stone and mortar. Enkidu dies, Gilgamesh suffers, but the city of Uruk flourishes. Since at the very start of the epic, the purpose of the encounter of the wild man with the civilized king was to restore justice to the city, the poem has, after all, a happy ending. The portrait of

King Gilgamesh at the very beginning of the poem offers
a clue:

> He had seen everything, had experienced all emotions,
> from exaltation to despair, had been granted a vision
> into the great mystery, the secret places,
> the primeval days before the Flood. He had journeyed
> to the edge of the world and made his way back, exhausted
> but whole. He had carved his trials on stone tablets,
> had restored the holy Eanna Temple and the massive
> wall of Uruk, which no city on earth can equal.

What the poet tells us is that, after the ordeals and
adventures, after the revelation and the loss, the king
must do two things: preserve the splendour of his city
and tell his own story. Both tasks are complementary:
both speak of the intimate connection between building a
city of walls and building a story of words, and both
require, in order to be accomplished, the existence of the
other.

All stories are our interpretation of stories: no reading
is innocent. The nineteenth-century decipherers of the
Nineveh tablets, George Smith and his colleagues, chose
to read the *Epic of Gilgamesh* as an endorsement of the Biblical account of Western society's beginnings. The core
tale of the epic, the questioning of a monarch's rights, had
for them little relevance. In Queen Victoria's realm, the
story of a king who learns humanity from a wild other,
and builds with him a powerful friendship, must have
seemed almost incomprehensible. When Rudyard

Kipling, in an effort to instruct his fellow Englishmen on the extent and variety of the British Empire, asked the question, "What should they know of England who only England know?" he wasn't being merely ironical. "Lo, all our pomp of yesterday," Kipling warned, "is one with Nineveh and Tyre!" — but Gilgamesh's Nineveh was not the one in which the English chose to see their mirror. Most of Victoria's subjects endorsed a definition of England based upon the exclusion of everything and everyone "not English." "Not English!" says the pompous Mr. Podsnap in Dickens's *Our Mutual Friend*, whenever he doesn't understand something, and with a wave of his arm dismisses the entire world outside his little sphere of knowledge.

Defined through exclusion, depicted as both foreigner and as mirror image, accused of both remaining a wild man and of never being able to become one with the acknowledged members of the city, Enkidu, in his many incarnations, continues to lead his suspicious existence simultaneously outside and within the city walls throughout the world. More than a century after the reign of Victoria, faced with a growing number of young British Muslims declaring their allegiance not to Great Britain but to the faith of Islam, Tony Blair's government decided to employ Mr. Podsnap's method and, in January 2007, decreed that schools were to insist upon the notion of "Britishness." That is to say, instead of allowing for an Islamic perspective to become part of the multiplicity of perspectives already intrinsic to whatever "Britishness" might mean (Saxon, Norman, French,

Scots, Irish, Welsh, Protestant, etc.), the government
decided to limit the concept of "Britishness" to a quality
of generalized local colour, of the kind employed in
tourist propaganda. To the concept of multiculturalism,
Blair's government opposed that of monoculturalism, in
which all cultures are supposed to blend indiscrimi-
nately but in which practically only the dominant culture
has a public voice. "What was wrong about multiculturalism," said Blair's chancellor of the exchequer, now
prime minister, Gordon Brown, using the past tense in a
demonstration of wishful thinking, "was not the recognition of diversity but that it overemphasized separateness
at the cost of unity." Brown proposed unity at the cost of
multiplicity, identifying a national "Us" as a means *not* to
identify with "Them" — whoever the other might be.
The point Brown missed is that it is not the "separateness" that is detrimental to unity, but the labelling of the
"separate" others as inimical.

Brown's attempt to define a national identity has been
echoed in several other countries, notably in France,
where the then presidential candidate Nicolas Sarkozy
proposed, on March 8, 2007, the creation of a Ministry of
Immigration and National Identity, thereby neatly cou-
pling in one institution what is to be walled out and what
is to be walled in. A wiser man than either Sarkozy or
Brown, active in an earlier multicultural society, that of
Alexandria in the third century B.C., proposed a different
way of considering the problem of "separateness."
Eratosthenes of Cyrene, employed in the great Library
of Alexandria, composed in his old age a philosophical

treatise now unfortunately lost but of which a few fragments have been preserved in the work of later writers. One of these fragments, quoted almost four centuries later by the geographer Strabo, has this to say about the notion of other: "Towards the end of Eratosthenes's book," says Strabo, "the author rejects the principle of a twofold division of the human race between Greeks and Barbarians, and disapproves of the advice given to Alexander, that he treat all Greeks as friends and all Barbarians as enemies. It is better, he writes, to employ as a division criteria the qualities of virtue and dishonesty. Many Greeks are dishonest and many Barbarians enjoy a refined civilisation, such as the people of India or the Aryans, or the Romans and the Carthaginians."

For Brown or Sarkozy, assimilation or exclusion are the only methods to ensure the survival of a society's identity. A social policy of open identity, in a society that accepts the measure of its own evolution, is in their eyes too dangerous because that society might then be transformed out of all recognition. From their perspective, Uruk will only be Uruk if Enkidu is not allowed to live as Enkidu within its walls. For them, the other must either renounce his own identity or remain forever alien to us: in fact, the other (as other) must not be allowed to be part of us, since union with that other is supposed to have terrible consequences. Sarkozy and Brown have co-opted the moral of certain ancient legends, according to which the mere presence of the double means certain death. We, of course, must never identify with the "other" side. We are the virtuous ones, and Eratosthenes's distinction must not be taken into account in our case; otherwise we might find ourselves among those accused of displaying negative and uncivilized qualities.

In 1886, barely fourteen years after Smith's cavorting in the rooms of the British Museum, Robert Louis Stevenson published *The Strange Case of Dr. Jekyll and Mr. Hyde*, perhaps the most accomplished of all stories about the multiplicity of identities, in which the terror of the other is made explicit as the terror of what is in ourselves. (Nicholas Rankin notes that it is not by chance that between the letter H for "Hyde" and the letter J for "Jekyll" is the letter I.) Four years later, Oscar Wilde explored the same notion in *The Picture of Dorian Gray*, but while in Stevenson the two separate selves converge in the end, back to their common source, the ambitious Doctor Jekyll, in Wilde, the never-aging Dorian and his decaying portrait are condemned on the last pages to two separate fates: that of a haggard, wizened Dorian and that of his youthful portrait. In both stories, however, it is suggested that our intimate fears of self-revelation require, in order to be exorcised, the expulsion of this unexplored identity, the banishment of the other, the "bad" other, to somewhere outside the city walls.

The *Epic of Gilgamesh*, instead, proposes a healing of these fears, a recalling of that which we are afraid to acknowledge, in order to work and live in its presence. Gilgamesh becomes a full individual only by joining forces with the wild Enkidu, so that the egotistical ambitions of civilized man become tempered by the wisdom of the uncivilized one, and the city, the place of social intercourse, acquires its identity by defining itself through a sort of conglomerate individuality. This is what centuries later will become defined as the Social Contract, the passing from a pre-governmental state of nature to one in which human beings benefit from mutual support. What the *Epic of Gilgamesh* suggests is twofold. On the one hand, that civilization must find in what lies outside whatever contrasts and enriches its social and cultural identity; on the other, that the community must be healed from its inner evils by setting up rules and regulations, and enforcing their obedience. Gilgamesh the tyrant becomes Gilgamesh the hero through the appearance of Enkidu the wild man. And Enkidu the wild man becomes Enkidu the unwitting civilizer, a citizen of Uruk subject to its laws. Gilgamesh is himself when he is with another; the city is itself by enclosing its citizens (including its king) within the circle of its legislation. Uruk is the physical catalogue of urban conquests with which the poem concludes its praise of the city: "the palm trees, the gardens, / the orchards, the glorious palaces and temples, the shops / and marketplaces, the houses, the public squares," all ruled by the same law — but, at the same time, it must not forget the wilderness beyond, where its laws hold no power. The identity of the city, because of the laws that define it, depends on some sort of banning or exclusion. The individual identity requires the reverse: a constant effort of inclusion, a story reminding Gilgamesh that, in order to know who *one* is, we need *two*.

In the sixteenth century, Michel de Montaigne attempted to understand the reasons that move us to be together, whether we be frighteningly different or attractively similar. In the Municipal Library of Bordeaux is a copy of Montaigne's *Essays* annotated in his hand, with corrections for the printer, which Montaigne kept by his bedside to revise it at his leisure. In the first book, in Essay 28, he had written about his relationship with Étienne de la Boétie, a dear friend who had died in 1563 at the age of thirty-three, and whose loss Montaigne had felt so deeply. "In the friendship of which I'm speaking," Montaigne says, "souls are mingled and confounded in so universal a blending that they efface the seam which joins them together so that it cannot be found." According to Montaigne, in this kind of relationship the separation between "I" and "the other" is not denied: each preserves intact his individuality and uniqueness; only that the "seam" that unites them, and which is consequently what divides one being from the other, "cannot be found" in the eyes of the observer: it remains undetected and therefore unlabelled, free from the possibility of prejudice. This distinct invisibility, this evident but indefinable "separateness" that links two individuals in affectionate concern for one another, is what a fluid, multifaceted society may strive for, not only between two but between all of its members. Before jumping to the conclusion that such relationships are impossible on so large a scale, let us ask: in what does it consist, exactly, this as-if seamless relationship? Montaigne confesses that he finds it impossible to give an answer: "If you press me to say why I loved him, I feel that it cannot be expressed." This is how the paragraph ends in the text of all editions of the *Essays*, up to 1588.

But then, in 1592, shortly before his death, Montaigne found a sort of an answer and scribbled it on the right-hand margin of the printed book. After "it cannot be expressed," he wrote in his elegant script, "except by replying, because it was him." That is to say, because of those qualities that identified his friend and yet remained ineffable, because of what lent him existence not because of their perceived difference but because of his intrinsic qualities. And then, a few days or months later, as if the full notion had suddenly been revealed to him, Montaigne added five more words in a hurried hand and in a different ink, so that today we can read the whole sentence as one single thought, luminous in its wisdom: "If you press me to say why I loved him, I feel that it cannot be expressed, except by replying, because it was him *and because it was me.*"

III.

THE BRICKS OF BABEL

". . . to lend a purer sense to the words of the tribe . . ."
— Stéphane Mallarmé,
"The Tomb of Edgar Allan Poe"

ON SEPTEMBER 12, 1918, the thirty-five-year-old Franz
Kafka, who for years had suffered from the tuberculosis
that would eventually kill him, refused to enter the sana-
torium to which his doctors wanted to confine him and
left instead for the village of Zürau, where his sister Ottla
lived. He had decided to spend there a few restful weeks;
he ended up staying for what he called "the eight happi-
est months of my life." Looked after by his sister, he felt
well and rested; he ate, slept, and read nothing but auto-
biographies, philosophical works, and collections of
letters in Czech and in French. A month after his arrival,
he began writing again: neither short stories nor a new
novel, but reflections, fragments of thoughts, aphorisms

that were eventually published in 1931, seven years after his death, by his friend Max Brod under the title *Meditations on Sin, Suffering, and Hope.* Among these fragments, two in particular seem to complement and almost contradict one another. The first, bearing the number eighteen in the manuscript now at the Bodleian Library in Oxford, reads: "If it had been possible to build the Tower of Babel without climbing it, it would have been allowed." The second is number forty-eight: "To believe in progress does not mean believing that progress has already taken place. This would not be belief." The first aphorism seems to say that it was not the building of the Tower of Babel that provoked the divine wrath, but the wish to reach Heaven now, in the builders' present; this wish (a form of faith, the second aphorism suggests) is condemned to be always enounced in the future tense. According to Kafka, the language in which we formulate our beliefs, in order to be effective, must carry us forward to something not yet accomplished.

The eleventh chapter of the Book of Genesis tells that the people of the earth who survived the Flood spoke all one and the same language. After the waters had receded, they travelled eastward from Mount Ararat to the land of Shi'nar, where they decided to build a city, and next to it a tower that would reach into the heavens. According to a medieval Jewish exegesis of the Biblical story, the promoter of the colossal task was Noah's grandson Nimrod, whose mad ambition was to invade the Kingdom of God. Nimrod's people were divided into three groups: the first wished to wage war in Heaven; the second, to set up idols there and worship them; the third, to attack the heavenly hosts with bows and arrows. To punish them all, God sent down his angels, telling them "to confound their language, that they may not understand one another's speech." "Thenceforth," says the anonymous commentator, "no one knew what the other spoke; one would ask for the mortar, and the other handed him a brick; in a rage, he would throw the brick at his partner and kill him. Many perished in this manner, and the rest were punished according to the nature of their rebellious conduct." Those who had wished to attack Heaven with weapons were set against one another with axes and swords. Those who had wished to install their idols were transformed into apes and phantoms. And those who had wished to wage war against God were scattered all over the earth, forgetting that they were all once siblings bound by a common tongue. That, we are told, is the reason why everywhere today there is strife. The medieval commentators add that the place where the tower once rose never lost its peculiar quality of granting oblivion and that, even today, those who go by it forget all they once knew. Like Kafka's notion of advancement, the building of Babel has no past.

Instead, the builders of Babel were punished with a present in which countless forms of speech made language itself a cause for division, distinction, and segregation. And yet, this curious notion, that a common language preserves while a multiplicity of languages destroys the social fabric may perhaps be read as something different from a mere penalty: less as a rejection of other tongues than as an awareness of the importance of finding a common means of communication, of understanding what the other says and of making ourselves understood — consequently, of the precious value of the art of translating experience into words.

But can we, however, through this art, undo the curse of Babel? All words require knowledge of the other, of the other's capacity to hear and grasp, read and decrypt a shared code, and no society exists without a shared language. The underside of Babel's myth acknowledges that living together implies using language to be with one another, since language is a function that requires both self-consciousness and consciousness of someone else, the realization that there is an *I* transmitting information to a *you* in order to say: "This is who I am, this is how I see you, these are the rules and transactions that hold us together across space and over time." And through the knowledge of that *you*, it may be possible, one day, to tell stories that will explain what we mean by "mortar" and what we understand by "brick."

Most of the time, we demand that our own language prevail. "You must understand me, even if I don't understand you," has been for centuries the colonizer's banner. Ireland, for instance, invaded by England for the first time in 1169, continued almost nine hundred years later to remain Barbarian in the eyes of its colonizer. For the English, Ireland was (as Carlyle wrote in 1849) an "ugly spectacle: sad health: sad humour: a thing unjoyful to look back upon. The whole country figures in my mind like a ragged coat; one huge beggar's gabardine, not patched or patchable any longer." Never either truly assimilated nor subdued, Ireland was conquered by the English not once but several times, the land confiscated and redistributed again and again, and the population brought to the verge of extinction. To justify its actions, England proclaimed itself as the law and order that mad Ireland needed, and demanded that the Irish recognize this truth. Dr. Johnson, for whom Ireland was a land only slightly less barbarian than Scotland, saw England's assumptions differently. Some time before the Act of Union between Ireland and England became operative in 1801, Johnson advised an Irish gentleman not to allow that union to take place. "Do not make a union with us, Sir," Johnson insisted sternly. "We should unite with you, only to rob you. We should have robbed the Scotch, if they had had any thing of which we could have robbed them."

The primary objective of the Act of Union was not to assist and improve the Irish but to bring them "more completely into subjection," placing the Catholic three-quarters of the population under the rule of the Protestant Church and Crown. The results were, as we know today, economic measures that starved a vast number during the Great Hunger of the mid-nineteenth century, the ensuing emigration of more than two million people, mainly to the United States, and the division of Ireland in 1920 between the North and the South. The act also sparked the religious slaughter known euphemistically as "the Troubles," during which, as in Babel, "no one knew what the other spoke." On May 9, 2007, after four decades of violence, the leaders of both sides agreed to share the government of Northern Ireland, offering for the first time in their history hope of a peaceful cohabitation. On the front page of most papers, the Radical Unionist Ian Paisley, Ireland's new First Minister, was seen laughing next to the IRA's Martin McGuinness, the new Deputy First Minister. And yet, a question stands. In a Babel such as this, before the resolution as well as in the days to come: what can be the function of the storyteller?

In 1978, the Irish writer William Trevor published a collection of short stories, *Lovers of their Time*, which includes a story called "Attracta." Attracta is a Protestant schoolteacher in a town near Cork. She is sixty-one years old. Both her parents died when she was a small girl, and now she lives alone in a house inherited from an aunt. One day, Attracta reads in the paper that a English girl has committed suicide in Belfast. The girl's husband, an army officer, had been murdered by the IRA. He had been decapitated, and his head had been sent to the girl's house in Surrey, inside a biscuit tin. Until the girl had opened the tin, she had not known that her husband was dead. In response to the terrible act, and as a gesture of courage and perhaps of anger, the girl had gone to Belfast and joined the Women's Peace Movement. But this gesture, publicly reported, had incensed the murderers, and seven of them had broken into her house and raped her. Immediately afterwards, the girl had killed herself.

The news haunts Attracta for weeks; the image of the dead young girl is always with her. In part, the dreadful story brings back the memory of her own tragedy: that of her parents' death, which, as she was told when she was eleven, was the result of a mistake, a bungled attack on British soldiers. It also brings back the memory of several people from her past: of a Catholic man and woman who had been kind to her and to her aunt, but who had somehow been involved in the training of the killers; and of a bigoted Protestant neighbour who had tried to make her hate all Catholics, telling her that they were monsters, and that she was always to think of them as her enemies. But above all, what haunts Attracta is a suspicion: that, all during her lifetime, even though she is a teacher, she herself has learned nothing and has taught nothing.

Attracta decides to tell the children in her class about the English girl and also about her own life. At first, the children respond conventionally, by saying to her that "stuff like that [is] in the papers the whole time." Attracta insists. Meticulously, she describes the circumstances of the murder — the number of bullets fired into the husband's body, the careful wrapping of the head — and then tells the children about the death of her own parents. She intertwines the stories with descriptions of her childhood and of what the town looked like years ago, when she was a girl. "My story is one with hers," Attracta explains to her class. "Horror stories, with different endings only." And after telling them of the English girl's suicide as she herself sees it in her mind's eye, as if she herself were going through the deadly movements, Attracta asks the children: "If she had only known that there was still a faith she might have had, that God does not forever withhold His mercy. Will those same men who exacted that vengeance on her one day keep bees and budgerigars? Will they serve in shops, and be kind to the blind and the deaf? Will they garden in the evenings and be good fathers? It is not impossible." And Attracta adds these final words: "I only hope she knows that strangers mourn her."

The bell rings and Attracta watches them go out into the playground, like Cassandra on the walls of Troy. "It had meant nothing when she'd said that people change. The gleam of hope she'd offered had been too slight to be of use, irrelevant in the horror they took for granted, as part of life. Yet she could not help still believing that it mattered when monsters did not remain monsters forever."

Monsters do not remain monsters forever. This is one of the revelations that stories offer us. Caught in words, transmitted through words, put forward to serve as the point of departure for reflection and dialogue, the monsters perceived beyond the pale of society's laws can suddenly be seen in all their tragic humanity, revealed not as creatures capable of monstrous acts because they are unlike us, but because they are very much like us, and capable of the same things. These are the facts, stories tell us, and these terrible events belong to our common circle of existence. These are not inconceivable, magically evil acts: they are acts of our flesh and blood, and flesh and blood can mourn them, and remember them, and perhaps (this seems impossible and yet it happens) one day even redeem them. Language has a powerful accounting capability.

Much as we may lament the fact, written language, when it appeared, more than five thousand years ago, is not the creation of poets but of accountants. It comes into being for economic reasons, to keep stock of facts: of possessions, commercial dealings, agreements of purchase and sale. It does not develop in order to increase social and economic efficiency but runs parallel to that increase and, once developed, it does not, by itself, create any new civilizations; rather it allows them to become aware of their developing identities. The relationship between a civilization and its language is symbiotic: a certain kind of society gives rise to a certain kind of language; in turn, that language dictates the stories that inspire, mould, and later transmit that society's imagination and thought.

It is not fortuitous that definitions of individual and community should appear as the backbone of our earliest stories. Stories are not merely the product of our experience told through the medium of language. They are also the product of language itself, and depend on the specific language in which they are told. In the case of the *Epic of Gilgamesh* discussed earlier, the language that gave birth to the poem was Babylonian, a dialect of Akkadian, a Semitic tongue related to Arabic and Hebrew, and utterly different from the earlier Sumerian language spoken by the real-life Gilgamesh who, historians tell us, ruled in Mesopotamia around 2750 B.C. *The Epic of Gilgamesh* depends, of course, on its author's imagination, but also, in its narrative essence, on the whys and hows of the formation of the Babylonian language. "It is," wrote the eminent historian Jean Bottéro, "as if an early age, still little gifted with speculation [the Sumerian period], was followed by one of maturity, urgency and depth of thought [the Akkadian-Babylonian period], in which the Mesopotamians expressed themselves with ease and craft." The difference Bottéro points out is one of quality, not of output: the encyclopedic writings, for instance, typical of the ancient Sumerian literature of early Mesopotamia, are hardly found in later centuries, when the Mesopotamians adopted the more reflective Akkadian language. The language of the Sumerians served well to narrate a complex cosmology in which the gods and goddesses were routinely allotted certain attributes and functions, but enjoyed hardly any history. It was only with the establishment of the Akkadian language, and later its offshoot, the Babylonian dialect, that questions about the origin of the world and the workings of the gods began to appear. By the time the *Epic of Gilgamesh* was written, these questions lay at the very core of Mesopotamian society, leading to myriad others concerning the duties and responsibilities of government and citizens, the role of fate in an individual's life, the notion of a national identity. In the older language, poets said: "This is who I am, this is who we are." In the newer one, which allowed them to dwell on the ambiguities of an open, interrogative form of thought, they turned their conclusions into starting points: "Who am I? Who are we?" Uncomfortable questions, at the best of times.

According to biologists (Richard Dawkins among others), the art of language, together with various specialized functions, began developing in living creatures when, as survival machines for auto-reproductive genes, they started to interact among themselves in order to influence one another's nervous system and social behaviour. Imagination itself, the ability to conceive a reality not materially present to the senses, is also a product of this interaction. A wonderful example of this process of invention is offered by the study of the song of birds. It is known that, when a hawk approaches a flock of feeding birds, one of the birds will utter a warning cry so that its fellows can escape the threat. In doing this, the vigil bird will draw the hawk's attention to itself and, in many cases, become the hawk's prey. In many cases, but not in all. Sometimes the hawk will not notice the bird and fly away empty-clawed. The vigil bird, forsaken by its comrades, is then left to feast on the fruit of the tree, all by itself, to its heart's content. If this instance repeats itself, then the bird will learn that, when it utters its warning song, the result may be a treeful of food and no competition. Thereafter, perhaps when food is not plentiful, it may try out its song even with no hawk on the horizon, exclusively for the sake of eliminating the other feeders. In doing this, the bird so to speak "lies," "makes up" a situation of danger, uses what, in human terms, we would call "imagination." It is, of course, a mistake, when speaking of birds and other non-human creatures, to use an anthropomorphical vocabulary, such as the verbs "to lie" and "to imagine," which imply literate self-consciousness, but the example nevertheless reflects a similar pattern among the individuals of the *homo sapiens* species. How did this pattern come into being?

Fully articulate human language is a recent development, barely some fifty thousand years old. Written language appeared much later still: the oldest examples of writing we have are from around the third millennium B.C. By then, the words fashioned by and for common use had acquired the power to fashion thought themselves. This astonishing notion, that words think us into being, that words not only express but create thought, was developed long ago, in the sixth century, by the Indian philosopher Bhartrihari. It deserves close attention.

In early social stages, when social groups came together only on those occasions when a shared need called for communality (to hunt or to share crops, for instance), written language consisted for the most part of pictures or ideographic signs, and depended largely for its interpretation on the imagination of the individual reader. Both the signs themselves and the style in which they were drawn carried a functional and a symbolic value. "Evolutionary functionalists" (as the specialists who study the development of language are called) have demonstrated that there is a strict separation between style and form — between the decorations on a pot and its shape and size, for example — since the former evolve by random process and the latter by selection. These scientists have confirmed what artists have long intuited: that style is vital to our comprehension of reality, and that how we depict or say something carries communal weight, a wealth of cultural connotations imprinted in our genetic capacity to understand certain codes. "In matters of grave importance," Oscar Wilde neatly put it, "style, not sincerity, is the vital thing."

During later developments, when agriculture and husbandry were organized around a community of settled craftsmen and administrators, and property (individual and communal) was considered the measure of a society's importance, it became essential that the rules and regulations to protect and define the interaction of individuals be taught and learned quickly. For that purpose, a code of phonetic, not pictorial signs, was developed to mimic oral language following shared conventions. The stories on the walls of Altamira are no doubt as powerful as those on the tablets of Nineveh, but while the former depend mainly on our private invention for their telling, the latter rely on a word-by-word translation, carrying, as accurately as possible, not only a narrative through line but a syntax and precise meaning, from the inscriptions of four thousand years ago into the words of our present. Perhaps to this increased ability to tell and preserve stories by means of variously new and improved technologies, our human evolution largely owes its accelerated pace.

The double virtues of language, its simultaneous powers of creation and transmission, are made explicit in the recognition that each of us exists in relation to another. Every story is a triangle made up of these binds: author and reader, reader and protagonist, protagonist and author. There is an author, such as Trevor, who appeals to his readers and projects his free-standing characters onto the world. There is a reader, you or I, who enacts the magic trick of conjuring up those characters, and who follows the story and grants it new meaning. There is a protagonist, such as Attracta, who comes to life and claims on the page equal status as that of her author and her reader. Each one of the three finds a reflection in the remaining two, and all three reflect the several ways in which the other is seen. Every literary relationship entails, more or less consciously, all three ways of seeing the other: as a fantastical being, quasi-fictional, who carries a symbolic or allegorical weight in our imagination; as a threat, as someone who covets our property and our identity, and whom we must fight and destroy; as a creative benefactor who will govern and teach us wisely, and whom we must court and love.

Readers create writers who in turn create readers. In this chicken-and-egg situation, each new reading and each new writing must teach its methods to its audience, present or future. The inability of Melville's contemporaries to read *Moby-Dick* or of Blake's to realize the extent of his artistic genius show how slow these teaching processes are. The expansion of literacy, from the days of Mesopotamian tablets to the electronic media of today, has allowed us to create memory banks vaster and more reliable than the human brain, that store away, for future use, these ongoing creations. This, of course, does not preclude the need to exercise our own memory, since recalling is not remembering, reading is not possessing texts, and (as the ancient librarians of Alexandria knew) the accumulation of knowledge is not knowledge. As our capacity to store experience increases, so does our need to develop keener, deeper ways of reading the encrypted stories. For this we need to leave aside the vaunted virtues of the quick and easy, and restore the positive perception of certain almost lost qualities: depth of reflection, slowness of advancement, difficulty of undertakings.

Likewise, writers sometimes require long periods of observation before creating a literature that illuminates their time, shedding light on the past and also the future, as memory or as warning. Sometimes great catastrophes, the First World War or the Holocaust, rapidly give rise to a universal literature. Erich Maria Remarque's *All Quiet On the Western Front* appeared in 1929. Primo Levi's stories *If This Is a Man* and Paul Celan's poem *Todesfuge* (in a Romanian translation) were both published in 1947. Other times, the echoes are slower. It took more than half a century for literature depicting the sufferings of the German civil population during the Second World War to find its audience with the publication of W. G. Sebald's *On the Natural History of Destruction* in 1999 and Jörg Friedrich's *The Fire* in 2002. In the countries of Latin America, the imaginative response to the centuries of tyranny gave rise to what one might call a specific literary genre. In 1968, Carlos Fuentes had the idea of compiling an anthology of fictional accounts of these dictatorships that he would call *Los padres de la patria* ("The Fathers of the Fatherlands"), and asked a number of novelist friends each to write about a dictator from their own country. They had, alas, what the French appropriately call *"l'embarras du choix."* Fuentes himself would write about General Santa Anna in Mexico, Miguel Otero Silva on Juan Vicente Gómez in Venezuela, Alejo Carpentier on Gerardo Machado in Cuba, Augusto Roa Bastos on José

Rodríguez de Francia in Paraguay, and Julio Cortázar on
Eva Perón in Argentina. Though the project unfortunately
never materialized, several writers took up his suggestion. Years later, Augusto Roa Bastos published *I, the
Supreme* and Gabriel García Márquez, whose native
Colombia was one of the few countries not to boast or
bemoan a notorious dictator, invented a composite figure
for his *Autumn of the Patriarch*.

The War in Iraq, for example, has not yet produced, in
the Arab-speaking world, its literature, except for a couple of novels by exiled Iraqi writers Mahmoud Saeed
(*Saddam City*) and Jinan Jassem Al-Halawi (*Hot Zones*).
The Iraqi poet Mohammad Mazloum has suggested that
perhaps it is imaginatively difficult to write about "a war
that opposes a dictatorship to an imperial power" and
that the few texts that have appeared on the subject are
less literary creations than expressions of circumstantial
emotions. The Syrian poet Abid Ismaïl believes that the
problem lies in the murkiness of the subject. "Writers fear
that they're between a rock and a hard place: if they condemn the war, they will be accused by many Iraqi and
Arab intellectuals of defending the dictatorship [of Sad-
dam]; if they justify it, they will be accused of favouring
the occupation." A number of Arab intellectuals echo
Ismaïl's concern: in a war that day by day increases the
bloodshed, the chaos, and the segregation of the people of
Iraq, a war in which no one seems to understand his
neighbour and over and over again mistakes mortar for
brick, no clear vision can emerge except the obvious conclusion that the killing must stop. Perhaps the silence

surrounding the War in Iraq is an expectant one, one that recognizes that no poetic answer is immediately possible.

The identity a writer grants a society stems from that which the language of that society inspires and determines; obviously, the degree of conflict under which that society lives (since every society is always in some measure of conflict) hinders or disarms the writer's attempts. Dictatorship, war, famine, colonial oppression, racial persecution, ethnic cleansing shatter the imaginative construction of our identities, undermine our sense of the past, work to prevent us from building Babel while at the same time demanding that future Babels be built. Any society requires laws curbing and regulating its citizens' ambitions, but the duty of the citizens is always to question these laws, to test them and work toward their improvement, and sometimes to undertake actions that lie outside the law's jurisdiction, such as Attracta's mourning and bearing witness.

In this exchange between braces and relaxes, between social order and rebellion against that order, on occasion, almost miraculously, we manage to reach with our bricks the higher circles of the tower, building out of whatever tools are there, in a medium or voice that seemed forbidden to us. We manage to create an inspired identity, an inspiring story, coherent and truthful, reflecting back to us a useful concept of reality in the renewed "words of the tribe" that Mallarmé demanded. The indigenous artists of South America who constructed their own syncretic visions in the baroque style learned from their Spanish and Portuguese masters; the

African slaves who drew from Biblical imagery and European liturgical music the components of their narratives and songs; the writers from the imperial colonies who in the tongues of the colonizer produced the literature that renewed and revitalized those same tongues — all are proof of the possible success of such banned undertakings. One such creation took place recently, in the Inuit territory of Nunavut.

Writing in 1987, the British author Sam Hall noted: "From Australia to the Americas, the image of the classic Eskimo is still that of Nanook of the North, the indomitable hunter clad in a sealskin anorak and polar-bear pants, his harpoon poised for the kill, his son lying happily with the husky puppies on the ice outside the family igloo. In the Arctic today, this vision is as ludicrous as that of Caesar, his toga flowing behind him, a bunch of grapes in one hand and a silver chalice in the other, striding through a traffic jam in Rome."

Nanook of the North was, of course, the protagonist of Robert J. Flaherty's 1921 silent film, subtitled "The Life of an Eskimo and His Family." *Nanook of the North* was a cinematic revolution, and if today we know that Flaherty set up and altered scenes in order to satisfy dramatic and technical requirements, attributing to an Inuit character the lineaments of a Western conception of landscape and story, the film is nevertheless a masterpiece. Sixty-six years later, Hall was right in noting the anachronism (if not the downright falsification) when placing the screen Nanook next to his fellows in the desolate reality of twentieth-century North America. Of Flaherty's vision, little withstood confrontation with the facts: instead of the happy, stalwart people Flaherty had depicted, the Inuit were dying out, unemployment was (still is) the highest in Canada, and the suicide rate among young people was soaring. Only on the screen did the Inuit live up to their adventure-story stature: even the real Nanook died a few days after the film was completed, of starvation, on the ice. Flaherty's film was a remarkable achievement, but in essence it remained a preconception, like Caesar and his flowing toga.

Eighty-five years after Flaherty's *Nanook*, another film on the identity of the Inuit was hailed as a masterpiece around the world. This time, the director was himself an Inuit, Zacharias Kunuk, and his film told an Inuit story, *Atanarjuat: The Fast Runner*. Something new, something that demanded a different receptive method for a different voice, was being shown, and, in the process, the audience was taught another way of seeing, a viewpoint from within the other culture itself. If Flaherty's film was an exquisite realization of something that he had convinced himself was out there on the infinite ice, while remaining nevertheless oblivious to the nature of that something, Kunuk's film, in a sense, corrected the focus, directing it beyond what Rudyard Kipling, in a poem in defense of the Inuit, had ironically called "the white man's ken." In *The Fast Runner*, Nanook's story has been taken back and translated into its original, forcing the audience to effect a cultural transmigration. *The Fast Runner* makes us watch not from the other side of the camera, but from the other side of the ice itself.

The Fast Runner tells the story of a nomad Inuit community that, in the distant past, is visited by an unknown shaman who brings discord to its inhabitants. A long time later, the curse finds its resolution in the conflict between Oki, the son of the group's leader, and two brothers, Amaqjuaq "the Strong One" and Atanarjuat "the Fast Runner." Atanarjuat wins the lovely Atuat from Oki; Oki seeks revenge by ambushing the brothers and killing Amaqjuaq. Atanarjuat tries to escape, running naked across the ice. But in the end, individual action alone cannot exorcise the curse. This can only be achieved through a remembering and understanding of the story and a recognition of its part in reality. Then, through the intervention of another shaman, without anger or thirst for revenge, by means a simple edict of exclusion, the society is healed. That which was brought in through the telling is rejected also through the telling. *The Fast Runner* is a film about story.

The Fast Runner is set at the beginning of the first millennium; for the viewer, this is comparable to "no time" or to the "once upon a time" of Western storytelling. Western convention dates time from an divinely decreed moment, whether the birth and death of a god or the travels of a prophet; for the Inuit, the narrative progression from before to after carries no such revelatory implications. Time, like space, is an area through which we move but in which our traces are effaced by that very movement. Progress (as Kafka believed as well) is a meaningless concept; we advance along a cyclical path in which events and the stage of these events appear and reappear as both cause and effect of any given happening. Perhaps for that reason, among the Inuit, space and time are not regarded as individual or even social properties, but as given areas in which we assume certain individual and social responsibilities, to ourselves and to the "social other," to the animals with whom the world is shared. Land and sky, sea and ice, days and nights, are individual beings, and belong to no one. Cairns are erected not to domesticate the landscape but to signal an ancient path that may serve as marker for a present-day migration. The poet Yves Bonnefoy, writing on Inuit mythology, noted that "in anthropomorphizing the natural environment and in establishing divisions between that environment and the social milieu, [this mythology] reflects and serves as the foundation for social order and customs." Here "connection counts for more than explanation," and *The Fast Runner* weaves all kinds of implied connections. No event, no act stands alone, nor does any individual or social element. The whole natural world is populated by a complex, dense story into which everyone and everything is woven, teller and listener included.

Only for an outsider, this world of ice appears empty, since there are no obvious signalizations here. It is the blank space on a map, the *terra incognita* that only imagination can fill. A legend has it that the name "Canada" was given to the country when the first Spanish explorers landed in British Columbia and exclaimed: "¡*Acá nada!*" ("Here's nothing!") A dumping ground of the Western psyche, a place of absolute exile, the great frozen spaces are the destination of Western society's rejects, from

Frankenstein's persecuted Monster to Jules Verne's adventurous Captain Hatteras. "The north focuses our anxieties," Margaret Atwood once said. "Turning to face north, we enter our own unconscious. Always, in retrospect, the journey north has the quality of a dream." This quality is not, however, opposed to wakefulness in the Inuit imagination: it is felt as complementary. For the Inuit, the ancient, universal metaphor of death as sleep (one of whose earliest appearances is in the *Epic of Gilgamesh,*) is perfectly true: sleep is death, death is sleep, and the dead inhabit our dreams in order to share with us their rightful territory. It is not by chance that one of the brothers, Amaqjuaq "the Strong One" must die; in this way, he and his brother, Atanarjuat "the Fast Runner," the living, may inhabit a world rendered complete.

Among the Inuit, the territories of wakefulness and of dreams are the only geography; landscape, instead, has no imaginative presence. It has been observed many times that the notion of landscape is an urban construct and that those who live outside city walls do not differentiate between an all-encompassing nature and a backdrop for human action. Shifting ground of breaking ice and falling snow, a horizon that melts and blends into the light or darkness above, the absence of constant features that give defining permanence to the lived-in world: all this dissolves for an outsider the acquired notion of space, as dreamspace dissolves the space of woken time. For Canadians, the greater part of the country, the frozen north, is, as Atwood suggested, mainly north in the metaphorical sense, the place within our borders toward that the country imaginatively heads in order to find itself. (Without our borders is another question.)

Northrop Frye famously wrote that the Canadian problem of identity was primarily connected to place, "less a matter of 'Who am I?' than of 'Where is here?'" Frye tells the now well-known story of a doctor friend who, travelling on the Arctic tundra with an Inuit guide, was caught in a blizzard. In the icy cold, in the impenetrable night, feeling abandoned by the civilized world, the doctor cried out: "We are lost!" His Inuit guide looked at him thoughtfully and answered: "We are not lost. We are here." This is something that, from the outside, we forget too often. There is here.

In *The Fast Runner*, "here" is identified with community, the grouping of people. Here is where men and women gather to eat, sleep, make love, and talk, the central point from which stories are told, the *incipit* — except that these stories belong to an ongoing narrative, constant in its unfolding and beginning again at every telling. Like other communal tasks, storytelling has the function of lending expression and context to private experiences, so that, under recognition by the whole of society, individual perceptions (of space and time, for instance) can acquire a common, shared meaning on which to build learning. Inuit history, says Bonnefoy, is one "in which many developments are merely implied or simply defined by their absence in accounts which apparently say nothing about them." The elusive notions of space and time, always implicitly present, when captured in a story, are granted, under a narrative shape, a particular identity that can be possessed by a group or individual. "A good line belongs to no one or to literature," Jorge Luis Borges noted, arguing, from a Western perspective, in favour of a worldwide anonymous literary creation. For the Inuit it is otherwise: the "good line," the "good story" is assimilated to the individual and social identity, and it belongs to them as much as (in Western terms) the land on which a house is built belongs to its dweller or the time allotted to work or leisure to each citizen. The story of *The Fast Runner* was therefore the property of the groups that had preserved it. In order to write the script, Kunuk and his Inuit crew interviewed eight elders from these groups who agreed to "give" him their version of the story, which was then recast by a mixed Inuit and Anglo-Canadian team. This permitted the story to be told both in cinematic language and in the language of Inuit narrative. By this means, story — allusive and nonlinear, visual and clipped into framed scenes — became *The Fast Runner's* shared currency.

In Western thought, place and time change hands and value. Territorial claims and conquests, real estate rights, time paid for, lost, killed, enjoyed, and sold per hour or per week, find their official manifestation in our sciences of geography and history. Within these spatial and temporal flows, our creative arts, however, are seen as immutable units, fixed in deathbed editions and framed in art museums. Western narrative demands from its audience the belief in a prehistory and a future beyond the page or screen, an extended pageant from which the story chosen has been cut. Published books claim for a work once printed a *nihil obstat*; Pierre Bonnard was arrested at the Musée du Louvre for attempting to retouch one of his own paintings; even works left unfinished at their authors' death are not allowed to be completed without an attendant scandal. In the Inuit imagination, it is place and time that remain constant as we travel through them: the stories, on the other hand, change in order to hold the passing of memory, since the telling of a legend is always both a voice from the past and contemporary of the teller. For a Westerner, it is difficult to leave aside the cumulative notion of time and accept that what is imagined and told as happening takes place in a constant moment that is, all at once, present, past and future. For the Inuit, it is the story, not time, that travels.

Movement, in time or space, is an act of resistance against passing: we move in order to remain. Running on the ice, naked, bleeding, the Runner makes no progress. This is the act of running in its archetypal state, since here there is no advancement in space and no progression in time. For a Western reader, such running echoes unwittingly other impossible attempts of escape, from the sublime to the ridiculous, from Dante's bleeding captain in Purgatory to Eliza on the ice floes in *Uncle Tom's Cabin*. Especially Alice in *Through the Looking-Glass*, who is told that she must run in order to remain still. "Well, in *our* country," Alice says to the Red Queen, who has forced her to run in order to *prevent* her from moving, "you'd generally get to somewhere else — if you ran very fast for a

long time as we've been doing." "A slow sort of country!"
the Queen retorts. "Now, *here*, you see, it takes all the running *you* can do, to keep in the same place."

This concept of an "active" story that allows us "to
keep in the same place" can be associated with Dawkins's
arguments mentioned earlier: in biological terms, imagination is a survival mechanism developed to grant us
experiences that, though not rooted in physical reality,
serve nevertheless to educate and improve with the same
power and efficacy as those that take place in the physical
world. We imagine (or dream, invent, and repeat) stories
that allow us to act out and record processes of learning
of which we may not be entirely aware, in a constant
interweaving between what happens in the world and
what we make-believe happens. In this sense, the story
materially lived out and the story lived out in the imagination hold equal ranks. Except that, in Western societies,
we grant the material stage a symbolic status of concrete,
solid value, and therefore claim for it proprietary rights,
while we relegate the imaginary constructs to unreality,
however amusing, terrifying, or illuminating we may feel
them to be. Søren Kirkegaard, whom Kafka was reading
during his time in Zürau, wrote in 1843 the following
Kafkaesque observation: "What philosophers have to say
about reality is as misleading as a sign found in a flea-
market, IRONING DONE ON THE PREMISES. You bring
your linen in and discover you've been fooled: the sign is
there for sale."

Memory, in Western experience, is our link to the
repositories of the past, along the streamline of time. In

Inuit terms, memory is exactly *equivalent* to present experience: that which is remembered *is* the reality in which we live, physically and imaginatively. There are no "stages" of knowledge and recognition in the act of remembering. We are that which previous experience has taught us, communally and individually (except that we must forego the notion of "previous"). The story that has been told exists only as the story told now. In this sense, film (the "modern" art) is the ideal medium for these ancestral recollections, since it grants them an immediacy that exists in the moment of being seen, adding vision to the quality of orality, making explicit the immediacy of memory. Or not memory, but memories, in the plural, because two memories compete for our trust. The memory of society that presents itself to us as continuous, coherent, and dogmatic, and the individual memory, chaotic, piecemeal, constantly challenged. In the world of *The Fast Runner*, the tension between both permits their co-existence and also grants them identity, and any infringement (the individual chaos crossing over into the societal order, for example) must be repaired by excision.

But by whom? Who is instrumental to this healing process between society and its individuals, in a non-progressive time and a non-mapable space? The French philosopher Michel Serres has usefully coined the term "*le tiers-instruit*," the "instructed third" or "troubadour of knowledge"; the Anglo-Saxons, as we have mentioned, called him the "maker." Serres uses this term to find a bridge between natural and human sciences, but it can be useful in finding such a bridge between the physical individual and the metaphysical society, between the experience of, for example, the Runner (confronted with threats from his amorous rival, with the murder of his brother, with the loss of the woman he loves) and his social group (that must hold the definition of itself within and beyond such individual considerations.) This is the role of the elder or, sometimes, of the shaman. The shaman, the "instructed third," with the help of an auxiliary spirit, can make his soul leave his body and dive (as did, according to legend, the first Inuit shaman) into a depth of darkness and light that allows him to repair the cosmic disorders produced by humans. All shamanic rites are carried out with the left hand, the looking-glass reverse of physical reality. To the complementary poles of individual and group, the shaman adds those represented symbolically by right and left, by reality lived and reality told, material world and the world of stories. A shaman brought the curse to the community in the first place; a shaman will help the community heal itself in the end.

At the core of *The Fast Runner* is a problem of narrative. Into a harmonious story, an element of discord is introduced that runs its course and produces a series of tragic events. Its resolution must be the restoration of order. In Greek, Judeo-Christian, or Islamic terms, stories are a divine gift or attribute: the gods, whether the Muse or the Holy Spirit, dictate or write the books. "To invite the gods, ruins our relationship with them but sets history in motion," says Roberto Calasso. And adds: "A life in which the gods are not invited isn't worth living. It will be quieter, but there won't be any stories. And you could suppose that these dangerous invitations were in fact contrived by the gods themselves, because the gods get bored with men who have no stories." The stories of *The Fast Runner* are most decidedly the stories of mortal beings. The curse is otherworldly, but the solution is of this world: a law that the community must decree to expel the evildoer to beyond the communal walls. Not as a private act of revenge, neither as a divine act, but as a social execution of justice among humans. This is an essential difference: in the Inuit tradition, the gods are present, but they are not narrative gods. In the beginning there is no word. In fact, there is no beginning. There is ice and darkness, and memory of that ice and darkness. And those, like the Inuit, are still here.

In 1936, Walter Benjamin published an essay, "The Storyteller," about the nineteenth-century Russian writer Nikolai Leskov, in which he maintained that the art of storytelling was disappearing, largely due to the rise of the bourgeois novel and to mass media. Stories, which for Benjamin were the instruments by which age-old wisdom was transmitted to contemporary society, were no longer sources of counsel. "If today," wrote Benjamin, "'having counsel' is beginning to have an old-fashioned ring, this is because the communicability of experience is decreasing . . . After all, counsel is less an answer to a question than a proposal concerning the continuation of a story just unfolding. To seek this counsel one would first have to tell the story . . . [since] counsel woven into the fabric of real life is wisdom."

Whether William Trevor's or Zacharias Kunuk's narrative strategies may be useful to heal a wounded society is a question that must remain open. Perhaps a story of the conflict between Catholics and Protestants (like the story of Greeks and Trojans) can serve as a reflection for many other of our present conflicts; perhaps the retelling of a legend that grants us knowledge of different concepts of time and space (such as those proposed by Kafka in his fables) may be useful to reimagine the necessary constraints imposed by our own. We know that conflicts are born from constructed perceptions of the other, from self-identifying dogmas that, out of fear of dissolution, exclude in order to better define, forgetting that those we see as monsters do "not remain monsters forever." Sometimes, as in *The Fast Runner*, society must resort to exclusion; other times, as "Attracta" argues and the recent events in Ireland have proven, inclusion may be the only way to put a stop to the conflict.

Ultimately, readers want to have words to name not the declaration of a dogmatic set of precepts, but legislations able to change with the growth of experience and enrichment of customs. They want words to name the comforts of peace but also the confusion, destruction, and desperation brought on by our ambitions. In all this, the various identities of tribe, language, religion, and philosophies may find common ground, because sometimes, the blanketing notion of a society's identity is in itself the cause of conflict. And then, rather than assemble our different characters, our various speeches, under a common but restricted language, it may be possible to interweave them all and turn the curse of Babel into a gift of many tongues. Like different readings, these interwoven tongues may illuminate our own circumstances (as in Kunuk's work) and also those of our neighbours (as Trevor does in his stories), beyond the notion of exclusivity or ownership. They may help us follow Kafka's advise of aspiring without concluding, building without climbing, that is to say, knowing without demanding exclusive possession of knowledge. I believe that we are still capable of such things.

IV.

THE BOOKS OF DON QUIXOTE

"Your hypothesis is possible, but not interesting," Lönnrot
answered. "You will reply that reality has not the least
obligation to be interesting. To which I will reply that real-
ity can forgo that obligation, but hypotheses can't."

— Jorge Luis Borges,
"La muerte y la brújula," 1942

ASPIRING WITHOUT concluding, building without climbing, knowing without demanding exclusive possession of
knowledge are different expressions of an ancient
dichotomy: that of reason against force or, as a medieval
commonplace has it, the battle between the practioners of
letters and the practitioners of arms. Perhaps the most
troubling version of this argument was penned in the

early seventeenth century by a tired man who had, in his youth, known the sufferings of war in Italy, had been wounded in the chest and left arm during the Battle of Lepanto, had spent five long years a prisoner of Algerian pirates, had returned to his native Spain where he had tried his hand with indifferent success at plays, romances, and poems, and then, in his fifty-eighth year, in the cell to which he had been condemned for reasons that remain uncertain, had dreamt up a bookish and impoverished old gentleman who decides one day to become a knight errant. Once a soldier, now a writer, well aware of the tribulations of both callings, Miguel de Cervantes Saavedra lent his Don Quixote, in the first part of the novel, a couple of speeches in which the knight compares the merits of letters to the merits of arms. Addressing a group of goatherds, Don Quixote reflects that in the idyllic days of yore, the use of force had not been necessary. "Happy age and happy centuries, to which the ancients gave the name of golden," he says to his bewildered audience, "and not because gold, which in our iron age is held in such high esteem, was in those lucky days obtained without any effort, but because the men who then lived were ignorant of two words, *mine* and *yours*." In that Golden Age, "everything was peace, everything friendship, everything harmony," and knights errant were not needed since strife and injustice were inexistent. But now, in "our detestable centuries," nothing and no one is safe, and therefore, to combat the "growing malice," the order of knights errant was fortunately instituted. Fine words and beautiful thoughts are no longer enough; weapons and physical strength are now required "to defend maidens, protect widows and help the orphans and the needy." Seamlessly, Don Quixote's praise of chivalry drifts into a praise of war, and the true purpose of war, Don Quixote explains, is to bring Christ's peace on earth, since letters require arms to protect the laws they pen. This unsettling justification has older echoes with which Cervantes was no doubt familiar. ⏌

After escaping from the ruins of Troy, holding his son's hand and carrying his old father on his back, Aeneas begins a voyage that, in Virgil's telling, will eventually take him to the starting place of Rome. Like every story that is told backward, from the author's present to that of his fictional creatures, Aeneas must repeat Ulysses's travels and fight once again the battle of the Trojans and the Greeks before he can plant the seed of the empire that will blossom in the time of Aeneas's creator, Virgil. During his many adventures, Aeneas, like his precursors, must also visit the Underworld, to draw from its venerable inhabitants confirmation of a noble destiny foretold. Aeneas's story, which includes and reinterprets those told by Homer, proposes a new order to the library of the world's classics. After Virgil, we remember differently, since now Troy's defeat is revealed as a postponed victory. The Trojan Aeneas will become the founder of the nation that will rule over the arrogant Greeks. That is now the new reading.

Though the emperor Augustus wanted Virgil to write something like a divine justification for his claims to the throne, the *Aeneid* is, of course, much more than an imperial panegyric. It is what Dante was to call, somewhat

extravagantly perhaps, a "fount of splendour" and many
readers after him "the greatest poem in the Latin tongue."
But it is also the story that granted Rome its identity, and
to Augustus an epic proof of his role as the empire's second founder. For these reasons, it was essential, as Virgil
recognized, that the superiority of the Trojans, that is to
say, of the future Romans, be made clear. Troy fell at the
beginning of history, as the incontrovertible testimony of
stories told since the time of Homer proved, but its fall
was not to be eternal. It would rise again — it had, in fact,
risen again — to shame its enemies and lord over all other
nations. To assert this truth, Virgil sought the fiery tongue
of Aeneas's dead father.

Led by instructions from the Sibyl, the future founder
of Rome descends into the Kingdom of the Dead, "darkly
under the lonely night amid the gloom." After crossing
various landscapes populated with all sorts of monsters
and prodigies, and meeting on the way some of the souls
of men and women he has loved, at length Aeneas
reaches a green vale where he sees his father, Anchises,
standing among a congregation of ghosts. Weeping for
joy, Aeneas tries to embrace him, but the old man is also a
ghost and flees from his son's grasp "like a winged
dream." Aeneas questions his father about the fate of the
dead, their punishments and their rewards. Anchises
answers him, but then changes the subject:

> Listen, for I will show you your destiny, setting forth
> The fame that from now shall attend the seed of
>   Dardanus.

Dardanus was the son of Jupiter, and ancestor of the kings of Troy, a distinguished lineage to which Aeneas brings that of his mother, Venus, goddess of love, and to which King Romulus, still to be born, will add that of his father, Mars, the god of war. Jupiter, Venus, Mars: from this prestigious stock, Anchises tells his son, Rome will be born.

> . . . great Rome
> Shall rule to the ends of the earth, shall aspire to the
>   highest achievement,
> Shall ring the seven hills with a wall to make one city.

What is this "highest achievement" that the old man announces? Anchises makes it clear: Rome's superiority will not lie in the pursuit of the arts, the fruits of love, the gifts owed to Venus, but in those of war, the terrible heritage of Mars. Anchises warns his son never to forget that, however magnificent the art and culture of other civilizations might be (namely of Greece, which the Romans greedily plundered), Romans are, and will remain, the true rulers of the world.

> Let others fashion from bronze more lifelike, breathing
>   images —
> For so they shall — and evoke living faces from marble;
> Others excel as orators, others track with their instru-
>   ments
> The planets circling in heaven and predict when stars will
>   appear.

> But, Romans, never forget that government is your
>   medium!
> Be this your art: — to practice men in the habit of peace,
> Generosity to the conquered, and firmness against
>   aggressors.

A curious claim for a poet to make, as Virgil and Cervantes were no doubt aware: that political power takes precedence over arts and culture. Many an imperialistic credo has been built on a similar argument, and Anchises's words have for today's readers a bitterly familiar ring. Deliberately or not, Virgil grants with these verses a road map for Rome's colonizing ambitions and for the ambitions of countless future Romes. We are stronger than others, Anchises tells his son and his descendants, and since strength is better than any art or science, we are entitled to the privileges of power, to conquer lesser breeds and lead our people in crusades against them. We are here to bring peace, whether that of Augustus or of Christ. We are the rulers (generous, just, and firm) appointed by the gods, and all others must obey us. Or suffer the consequences.

Rome, Christian Rome, launched its last crusade against the Arabs in 1270. More than two centuries later, Catholic Spain officially divested itself of its Arab and Jewish cultures, expelling both Jews and Arabs from its territory. With these acts of expulsion, in which the West attributed to itself the role of victorious overlord whose "medium" was "government," and to the Orient that of subservient enemy well versed in arts and crafts, the Arab and the Jew became, in the official view, the exotic other. However, in spite of the expulsions, Arab and Jewish thought continued to permeate every strand of Spain's "cleansed" society. As in the case of most decreed exclusions, Spain could not (and has not) been able to divest itself of those cultures that gave it a large part of its vocabulary, place names, architecture, philosophy, lyric poetry, music, medical knowledge, and even the game of chess. Though the Arab and Jewish presences were banned, Spanish society found secret ways still to retain the ghosts of its severed identities.

On January 2, 1492, the Catholic king Fernando of Aragon and queen Isabel of Castile entered Granada ceremonially dressed in Moorish clothing and, having agreed on the terms of the act of capitulation of the last of the Nasrid kings, Boabdil, settled in the Moorish palaces of what had been a Muslim city for more than two and a half centuries, in the heart of Moorish Spain, known as al-Andalus. Though before the capitulation the monarchs had assured Boabdil that the Muslims of Granada would be protected and allowed to preserve their customs, the mosques were quickly consecrated as churches and the use of Arabic forbidden: anyone found reading books in Arabic was considered a non-Spaniard and subject to heavy penalties.

The Jews were the first to be expelled. A few months after the capitulation of Granada, the king signed a decree ordering the final expulsion of the Jews, who, clinging to their Spanish identity, took with them into their North African and Palestinian exile the Spanish language, or a

form of it, called Ladino, to distinguish themselves from
the Arabic- or Hebrew-speaking others. Arabs and Jews
had enjoyed a long history on the Spanish peninsula. Legend had it that the first Jewish communities had
established themselves here at the time of the destruction
of the First Temple of Jerusalem, in 587 B.C., but archeo-
logical evidence points rather to the first century A.D. For
the Jews, Spain was the land promised to them in the
Bible, in a prophecy by Obadiah: "and the captitvity of
the Jerusalem, which is in Sepharad, shall possess the
cities of the world." Though modern historians associate
Sepharad with Sardis in Turkey, for the Jews Sepharad
has always been the Spanish homeland where they lived
for at least fourteen centuries, mingled with the rest of the
population as merchants and doctors, peasants and
landowners. Anti-semitism, barely noticeable during
Roman times, took root in Spain after the conversion of
the Visigoth king Recaredo to Catholicism in 589 and
reached its cusp almost nine centuries later, with the
decree of expulsion of 1492.

For the Arabs, the measures were somewhat different.
In the case of the Jews, the Catholic kings had imagined
that an edict of absolute expulsion would induce the Jews
to convert. A few Jews, in order to stay in Sepharad, did
indeed become "New Christians" and were given the
opprobious name of "Marranos," meaning "hogs." But
when the Arabs' turn came, the Catholic kings decided to
make the conversion option explicit; therefore, when the
decree to expel the Arabs was issued four years later, in
1502, it included an article exempting from exile all those

who agreed to enter the welcoming arms of the Mother Church. The Arabs who converted became known as "Moriscos."

The Arabs had arrived from North Africa eight centuries earlier, in 711, invading the Visigoth realm of the Christian king Rodrigo. Shortly after the invasion, a story began to take shape in a number of chronicles that imagined a sort of prehistory for the event, embellished with fantastical foreshadowings and prodigious happenings that offered proof of the Arab right to conquer the Christian kingdom. In the ninth century, the historian Ibn al-Qutiyya, a Muslim descendant of the Visigoth king Witiza, shaped the main legend into the following story:

> It is said that the Visigoth kings had a palace in Toledo, in which was a sepulchre containing the Four Evangelists, on whom they swore their coronation oaths. The palace was greatly revered, and was never opened. When a king died, his name was inscribed there. When Rodrigo came to the throne, he put the crown on his head himself, which gave great offence to his Christian subjects. Then he opened the palace and the sepulchre, despite the attempts of the Christians to prevent him. Inside they found effigies of four Arabs, bows slung over their shoulders and turbans on their heads. At the bottom of the plinths was written: 'When this palace is opened and these images are brought out, a people of their likeness will come to al-Andalus and conquer it.' That is why Tariq entered al-Andalus on Ramadan 92 [June 711].

Stories breed stories. Just as the Arabs had invented
stories such as that of al-Qutiyya to justify their conquest
as a divine event, the Catholic kings seized upon other
stories that explained the recapture of al-Andalus as the
execution of the will of God. For Catholic Spain, the Arab
invasion of the eighth century had been a punishment for
the sins of King Rodrigo and of his people, akin to the
flood God had sent to wash the world of its turpitude.
According to the Spanish version of the events, God had
decreed as Rodrigo's punishment not only the loss of his
kingdom but a horrible death as well: Rodrigo was condemned to be devoured by dragons sent by the Devil,
crying out, the old ballads had it, "I am eaten, I am
eaten, / there where my sin was the greatest!"

However, after eight centuries of Moorish domination,
God had seemingly decided that the time had come for
the punishment to come to an end, and for His kingdom
to be again of this world, settled forevermore on the
Spanish peninsula by faithful Catholic folk. But in order
for God's will to be done, Spain was to be cleansed of
heretics and be no longer either Sepharad or al-Andalus
but a pure Christian realm. Accordingly, distrust of the
converts began to grow among the old Catholic population. Marranos and Moriscos were accused of murderous
acts and treacherous behaviour, and in many places there
were terrible outbursts of violence against them. The conflict was largely a question of historical priority.
According to the Church, Spanish Christians had inhab-
ited Spain long before the arrival of either the Arabs or
the Jews, since everyone knew that the apostle James had

set foot in the Spain shortly after the death of Christ and preached the gospel here. The peninsula was therefore to become once again as pure as it was when in the hands of its original Christian inhabitants.

Christian and Arab stories justifying a perceived identity competed for authenticity, and in some cases shared a common narrative, though not, of course, the same reading. Among the stories apparent in these prehistories was one about the many precious objects that the Visigoth Christians had supposedly buried when news of the Arab invasion reached them: according to the Arabs, they had done this because the treasures were ill-gotten gains hoarded by infidels; according to the Christians, because they were relics that the pious wished to save from heathen hands.

It is therefore hardly surprising when, in the spring of 1588, at the height of the protest against the converts, a curious lead box was discovered in Granada, among the ruins of a crumbled minaret, in the site proposed for the enlargement of the Cathedral of the city. It contained two pieces of linen, a small wooden board on which was painted the Virgin Mary in oriental dress, a piece of bone, and a roll of parchment with writing in Arabic, Greek, Castilian, and Latin. An inscription revealed that the bone belonged to Saint Stephen, the first Christian to be martyred for the sake of his faith. The parchment itself, according to the translators called upon to decipher it, contained a letter by Saint Cecil, the legendary first-century archbishop of Granada. The letter explained that Cecil, being afflicted with blindness, had travelled from

Jerusalem to Athens. Shortly before reaching his destination, he had touched his eyes with a cloth, the same cloth found in the box, which proved to be the one used by the Virgin Mary to dry her tears during the Passion. Miraculously, Cecil found himself cured. He then discovered a Hebrew text translated into Greek by a disciple of Saint Paul. Dutifully, Cecil proceeded in turn to translate the prophecy from Greek into "the tongue used by the Christian people of Spain." The parchment then gave Cecil's version, a text written in Arabic script that prophesized among other things the coming of a Dragon from the North and a powerful king from the East.

"The tongue used by the Christian people of Spain": the declaration in the letter was momentous. If the document was authentic, then Saint Cecil, contemporary of Christ and founder of the Church of Granada, had spoken and written, not in one of the Biblical tongues, but in Arabic, and Arabic was therefore among the oldest languages of the peninsula, dating from at least the first century A.D. Most importantly, the Moriscos, the "New Christians," could now claim a Christian ancestry in Spain that was even older than that of the oldest Spanish Christians.

This startling revelation was to receive further weight with a second and even more important discovery made seven years later, in 1595, on the hill of Valparaiso, later known as Sacromonte, outside the walls of Granada. Here, a team of masons, restoring a fallen tower, discovered a number of lead disks inscribed with strange letters that seemed to combine Arabic, Latin, and Greek script with characters from a language no one had ever seen before, and which hastily summoned scholars assumed to be ancient Hispanic. More than two hundred lead disks (which came to be known as the *libros plúmbeos,* or "leaden books") were unearthed at the site between February 21 and April 10, 1595.

The new translated texts proved to be even more surprising than that of the parchment. According to what could be deciphered, during the reign of the Emperor Nero, in the first century A.D., two worthy Arabs, Ibn al-Radi and his brother Tesifón, were miraculously healed by Jesus Christ Himself, after which Tesifón received from Christ's own lips the name Cecil. This then was the origin of one of Spain's earliest saints, patron of the city of Granada: Saint Cecil, true Christian if there ever was one, had been astonishingly a Moor! Afterwards, filled with missionary zeal, St Cecil and his brother accompanied the Apostle James to Spain. James went on to Compostela, Cecil to Granada, and here, on the Sacromonte, the converted Moor engraved the leaden books and buried them, to be resurrected at the end of time, when Christianity would have need of them. Cecil's words would then be presented to a Church assembly that was to include Arabs as well as Christians, "and woe to him," the text warned "who will not accept them as true!"

What these startling texts suggested was that the Morisco minority belonged at the very heart of the Spanish nation. Arabic, not Latin nor Castilian, had been the first language spoken on the peninsula. Granada, not Compostela nor Toledo, was the cradle of the Spanish Christian Church.

The translation contained further revelations: that in the caves of the Sacromonte lay several of the first Christian martyrs of Spain who had met their blessed end at the hands of Nero's centurions in the fiery pits of quicklime (which can be visited to this day); that Christians would do well to pay attention to the holy texts of the Arabs, since the words of Christ and those, still in the future, of Muhammad, had curious and meaningful similarities; finally, that a highly controversial point of Catholic dogma, a point defended by the king of Spain's theologians but on which the Church of Rome remained skeptical, was to be embraced as true: the Immaculate Conception of the Virgin Mary, "untouched," the disks proclaimed, "by the first sin."

More findings followed in 1596 and 1597. The final discovery, in 1599, was of a box containing an icon of Saint Cecil which, the inscription said, guaranteed the authenticity of all the earlier documents. Unfortunately, this last finding was so obviously fake that it cast serious doubts upon all the previous ones.

Perhaps the most ardent defender of the authenticity of the leaden books was the newly appointed archbishop of Granada, Pedro de Castro Cabeza de Vaca y Quiñones. An erudite man who had studied philosophy and classical languages in Salamanca, Pedro de Castro had acted in official Church capacities in Granada for many years, until at last he was appointed archbishop of the city in 1589. Shortly after his appointment, he began devoting himself to the construction of a religious monument on the heights of the Sacromonte: an ensemble of buildings centred around a vast church that, in Pedro de Castro's mind, was to surpass in magnificence the heathen Alhambra that rose as an affront to the Christian world on the opposite hill. On the construction of the Sacromonte, Pedro de Castro spent not only the great majority of the Church allocations, but also his own private fortune. Every hour, every coin, every resource and effort the archbishop dedicated to his vast project that, on the one hand, was to be a monument to the glory of the Church of Granada and, on the other, an offering of thanks for the divine revelation of the leaden books.

The translated prophecies had announced that a "powerful king" would arrive to change the fortunes of the Church. Pedro de Castro felt that the words could have only one meaning: for "king," the translators should read "archbishop" or "king of the Church." And Pedro de Castro intended to see that the prophecy had not been uttered in vain. In the archbishop's view, since Granada was obviously the site of Spain's earliest Christians who had heard the truth from the lips of the Saviour Himself, it was Granada's sacred mission to defend Christianity against all temptations and threats. And just as obviously, he, Pedro de Castro, was the chosen leader in this holy fight, and the relics and leaden books were the rightful property of Granada. Even at the king's request, he refused to allow the disks out of his hands and when, in 1610, in order to force him to leave Granada, he was appointed to the archbishopric of Seville, he took them with him in a leather pouch that never left his side.

In fairness to Pedro de Castro, the earliest verdicts

decreed the finds to be authentic. Barely five days after
the unearthing of the leaden books, a Junta Magna was
assembled, composed of highly eminent Church scholars:
it is thought that Saint John of the Cross, who was living
in Granada at the time, was present at the debates. A fort-
night later the Junta pronounced a favourable opinion.
Immediately afterwards, theologians and linguists began
the hard work of deciphering the mysterious writing.
Among the most notable of the experts were two erudite
Moriscos, Alonso del Castillo and Miguel de Luna, who
had already tried their hand at translating the parchment
found in 1588. After the Junta had given its approval,
Alonso del Castillo wrote to Pedro de Castro, reminding
him of the time in which he had been in de Castro's service, criticising his colleagues (who lacked, he said,
"Arabic erudition") and proposing himself and de Luna
as translators of the texts. By 1592, the two colleagues had
prepared the version of the parchment's prophecies that I
summarized earlier.

Who were these two learned translators? Del Castillo
was the son of a new convert and a graduate from the
recently created School of Medicine of Granada. Fluent in
Arabic, he had been in charge of rendering into Castilian
the Arabic inscriptions of the Alhambra, and had also
been employed as interpreter by the tribunal of the Inquisition itself. During the War of Granada against the Turks,
he was in charge of deciphering intercepted documents
and of faking others to incite the enemy to surrender.
Because of his merits, he had been appointed by King
Philip II to catalogue the Arab books in the royal library

of El Escorial and to seek out others throughout the kingdom. Of Miguel de Luna, who may have been del Castillo's son-in-law, we know very little, beyond the fact that he was employed for a time as the king's official translator.

Miguel de Luna and Alonso del Castillo's endorsements of the finds did not go uncontested, and a number of other scholarly voices arose to criticize the leaden books' authenticity. These contrary arguments proved however unsuccessful, since the stakes for judging the documents real were far too high. Granada and its archbishop needed them to be authentic, and popular devotion wanted them to be true. Soon the Sacromonte was flooded with devout processions, crowded demonstrations of religious fervour, and reports of sudden miracles. The relics themselves were said to give off a mysteriously sweet fragrance, and strange lights were observed in the sky above the church, while the ghosts of ancient nuns and priests were seen to parade up and down the sacred hill at sunset. To support his Morisco experts, Pedro de Castro commissioned further translations, bribing (some said) impoverished scholars so that they would render a version concordant with the archbishop's taste.

The view from Rome was a different one. For the Pope and his advisers, the leaden books were most likely forgeries, though the relics themselves were thought to be authentic: a convenient assessment since it was deemed important that the Church of Granada, which until then had lacked any important holy treasures, should be

allowed to possess at least a few. The leaden books were
another matter. In the vocabulary of the Church, the discovery of holy relics is known as an "Invention," as in the
"Invention" or unearthing of the True Cross in fourth-
century Jerusalem, by the Emperor Constantine's mother,
Queen Helen. The term *Invention* allows a happy association between the unearthing of prodigies and the
fabrication of a fiction or a story, suggesting something
different from a pure fake since it concerns not merely the
construction of something to be passed off as real, but the
creation both of the object itself and of its attendant circumstances. The Church of Rome considered the leaden
books to be not an "Invention" wth a capital *I*, but, in the
lesser sense of the word, something "invented": a trick-
ery, a forgery, an attempt at grave deceit.

But, if the leaden books were fakes, who was responsi-
ble for faking them? Was it scholarly Arabs, wishing to
undermine the Christian Church? Was it Old Christians
with a vested interest in the Church of Granada and the
dogma of the Immaculate Conception? Was it the ever-
present militants of the Reformation, sworn enemies of
the Catholics? Was it Islamic proselytizers who wished to
advertise the prophecies as a happy foreshadowing of the
triumph of the Prophet's religion?

In 1619, the Inquisition brought to court an erudite
Morisco who told the holy tribunal that he wished to
retranslate the leaden disks. God, he said, had entrusted
him with the task of reading and interpreting "the
tongue-tied books of the Sacromonte," and he wished for
permission to pursue the divine command. The man was

familiar with the tribunal of the Inquisition. Years earlier, he had been accused of making herectical statements: denying the sacrament of confession, declaring that the Virgin Mary loved the Moorish nation above all others on earth, and disbelieving in Hell since, he said, God in his infinite mercy would not have created a place in which punishment lasted forever. The name of the prisoner was Alonso de Luna, and it was revealed that he was none other than the son of Miguel de Luna, co-translator of the documents.

Miguel de Luna, the father, had died in 1615, a faithful servant of the Church and the king. His son, Alonso de Luna, was now charged with heretical pronouncements. The tribunal was asked to determine whether the accused was mad or pretending to be mad, and to that effect Alonso de Luna was led into the torture chamber. Barely after crossing the threshold, he cried out in fear and begged to make his confession: that Arabic was his mother tongue, Islam his religion, and that his secret intention was to convert Granada to the faith of Muhammad. Condemned by the tribunal to prison, Alonso was reconciled with the Catholic Church in an *auto-da-fé* celebrated barely a year later.

But the essential question remained unanswered: if Alonso de Luna, an unbeliever, had declared such great interest in deciphering the leaden books, to serve, no doubt, his heretical principles, could he not also have been the author of those same documents? Could he not have made up the prophecies that his father was later to reveal to the world? The tribunal of the Inquisition gave its verdict: after careful investigation, the venerable judges decided that the responsibility for the forgeries lay on the shoulders not of the son, Alonso, but of the father, Miguel de Luna and of his partner, Alonso del Castillo. According to the Inquisition, the men who had translated the mysterious documents were also those guilty of having created them. Sir Arthur Conan Doyle could not have imagined a more ingenious plot. Though the accusation was never proven to the satisfaction of every scholar, modern historians tend to agree with the verdict of the Inquisition: perhaps because, if nothing else, the idea of a forger being the interpreter of his own forgery has a certain literary elegance that is aesthetically pleasing.

Pedro de Castro died in 1623. In 1632, by order of the king, the books were sent to Madrid from where they were eventually remitted to the Vatican. Here they remained under lock and key until the year 2000, when the ultra-conservative bishop of Granada and ardent believer in the truth of the prophecies managed to convince his friend, the then Cardinal Ratzinger, to return the books, the parchment, and the other relics to his city, where they were received with great fervour and pomp. Today a few of the books can be seen on display at the Museum of the Sacromonte, a startling proof of the power of a story.

But what exactly was this story, made up of bones and cloth and parchment and strange words in various coded scripts inscribed on dark leaden disks, like something out of a Boy's Own adventure? What does it tell about the segmented country in which it took place? What argument is it proposing? Nineteenth-century historians saw in the mysterious documents an attempt by the Morisco population of Spain to integrate the faith of Muhammad with that of Jesus. Probably the faked documents stemmed from a messianic impulse, from the will of the Moriscos to take on an active role as the bringers of light to the Christian faith — a faith that was expelling them from their Spain, a faith that, fearful of competition, seemed to be crumbling under the weight of blind dogma and the rigid bureaucracy of Philip II, known as "the paper king" because of his love of red tape.

But the Old Christians of Spain saw the matter differently. Clearly the Moriscos, the so-called New Christians, were not to be allowed to succeed in their attempt at co-option. Clearly the only solution was to do away with their threat. Courtiers, clergymen, and the military convinced Philip II's son, Philip III, that the Moriscos represented a serious danger for the stability of the realm. On April 4, 1609, the king signed a new decree, this time banning all Moriscos from the Spanish territory. In September began the long exodus of the Moriscos of Valencia, Granada, Aragon, Catalunya, and Castile, and finally those of the Valley of Ricote, in Murcia, in the early months of 1614. In all, more than three hundred thousand Spanish Moriscos were made to leave their homes and travel to the unknown lands of North Africa, from where their ancestors had come more than nine centuries ago.

Four years before the new decree of expulsion was signed, in 1605, *The Ingenious Knight Don Quixote of La Mancha* was published in Madrid. The curious book

presented itself not as the original work of the author
whose name appeared on the cover, but as a translation
from the Arabic. "Though it may appear that I am the
father of Don Quixote," wrote Cervantes in his foreword,
"I am but his stepfather." The novel famously begins by
telling the story of an old man who, influenced by novels
of chivalry, decides to become a knight errant. But after
only eight chapters, in the middle of an adventure, Cervantes confesses that he doesn't know what happens next
and that he must abandon his hero halfway through a
battle: the baffled reader is left in the middle of a page,
thirsting for the outcome.

Cervantes then goes on to explain that, finding himself
one day in a busy street of Toledo, he sees a pile of manu-
scripts that attracts his attention. Since he is an addict of
words and will read even pieces of torn paper in the
street, he decides to buy the lot, though he can see that it
is written in Arabic characters, which, of course, he can't
decipher. Curious to know what the pages contain, he
looks around for a Moor who might be able to translate it
for him. In Cervantes's Spain, though officially the Arabic
and Jewish cultures no longer exist, everyone knows that
among the converts, there are still many (and easily
found, Cervantes notes, both Arabs and Jews) who still
speak the banned languages, including Aljamiado, a
romance language closely associated to Spanish but written in Arabic script. Cervantes chooses his man and asks
him for a quick translation. The Morisco glances through
the manuscript and bursts out laughing, and explains
that he has just read that "Dulcinea del Toboso, so often

referred to in this story, was the best hand at salting pork in the whole of La Mancha." In order to share the joke, the reader needs to know two things: that Dulcinea is Don Quixote's wishful beloved and that Toboso was a town famous for the number of Moriscos, and who certainly would not (in spite of the professed conversion) have anything to do with pork. The translator then reveals to Cervantes that the manuscript is *The Story of Don Quixote of La Mancha*, written by a certain Cide Hamete Benengeli, Arab historian. Delighted, Cervantes invites the Morisco to his house where, for a fee of fifty pounds of raisins and a hundred of wheat, he will translate the manuscript into Spanish. (Alas, then as now, translators were paid miserably.) The translation takes six weeks: the book the reader holds in his hands is the happy result.

What has happened? Against the official censorship, against the strictures of the Inquisition and the laws of ethnic cleansing, the presence of the banned cultures is acknowledged in Cervantes's novel as thoroughly alive and fruitful. With an astonishing sleight-of-hand, Cervantes manages to present his book as the work of an exotic author, a once Spanish, now outcast Moor, the rejected other. Dozens of translations followed the novel's success in Spain and *Don Quixote* quickly became one of the world's most popular books, so that, what would eventually be considered Spain's emblematic masterpiece and the acknowledged symbol of its culture, was read around the world as a supposedly Arab creation, the "invention" as it were of a people condemned to live outside Spain's walls.

Not that *Don Quixote* is entirely free of anti-Arabic prejudice. Cervantes's characters share the national sentiment against the Moor and several times the stereotypical negative attributes of the Arabs are invoked, if only as if sharing the putative reader's assumptions. "If any objection might be made to the truth of this story," Cervantes writes, to buttress his own literary fiction, thereby forestalling any doubts the reader might have as to its truth, "it can only be that its author is Arabic, since it is proper of that nation to lie." And yet, at the same time, there is a deep recognition of the loss of that vast area of almost millennial Spanish identity.

Six years after the signing of the decree that banned the Moriscos from Spain, in 1615, Cervantes published Part II of *The Adventures of Don Quixote*. In the fifty-fourth chapter, Cervantes introduces to the reader an old neighbour of Sancho's who bears the revealing name of Ricote, the last town from which the Moriscos were exiled. Ricote is himself an exiled Morisco who has returned to Spain disguised as a pilgrim, in order to recover some goods he has left buried in their village. Ricote tells Sancho that he and his fellows were not made welcome in North Africa, and that abroad, wherever they find themselves, they weep for Spain, "since here we were born and since here is our natural homeland." Ricote has been expelled from the land he calls his own: the description of his exodus, and later that of his family, his longing for his rightful homeland and his claims against the injustice of his exile, echo strongly for today's reader to whom the media bring daily news of similar expulsions and sufferings.

But Cervantes never depicts his characters one-sidedly and Ricote has all the ambiguities of the outcast, convinced that his imputed faults justify his condition as victim. Movingly, Cervantes has Ricote acquiesce to the unjust royal measure: Moriscos, he acknowledges, are indeed a threat to Christian Spain. "I was forced to believe in this truth through my knowledge of the vile and senseless intentions of our people, and I now believe it was divine inspiration that led His Majesty to put into effect such a gallant resolution, not because all of us were guilty, because some were true and stalwart Christians, but so few that they could not oppose those who were not, and it wasn't right to nurse a viper in one's bosom, or to keep enemies inside the house. Finally, we were condemned with just reason to exile, a soft and mild punishment in the view of some, but in ours the most terrible that could have been dealt us." In spite of the justifying arguments, Sancho (as well as the reader) is left with the sense of how "terrible" the punishment really is. Ricote is part of Spain, Cervantes seems to say, and if we are to be our true selves, then we must accept that we are also what we have expelled and branded. For Cervantes, that which we see as alien is merely ourselves condemned to exile.

Cervantes and his other, Cide Hamete Benengeli, are reflected in turn in a further pair of doubles: their fictional creations, Don Quixote and his squire, Sancho Panza, who begin their adventures as two utterly opposing personalities, but end as two intermingled characters, like Gilgamesh and Enkidu. By the end of Part I, Don Quixote has shown some of Sancho's practical materialism and Sancho has learned a little of his master's ideals of justice. They have become ennobling mirrors set face to face, reflecting the qualities that, invisible in one, are apparent in the other, and vice versa. Back from their adventures, the knight and his squire are greeted by Sancho's wife. "What good has come of your squiring? What dresses do you bring me? What shoes for your children?" "I have nothing of that kind," Sancho answers with a conviction that echoes that of his master. "But I bring with me other things more momentous and important." Sancho does not list them, except the joy of adventure itself, but the reader understands that Sancho has acquired from Don Quixote a different sense of justice, universal and absolute, which maintains the importance of acting fairly in an unfair world, not as conquering soldier but as a mere noble human being, whatever the consequences. And Sancho has acquired from his master a different sense of reality as well. During his passionate speech on the rival merits of arms and letters, Don Quixote says: "Indeed, my lords, if well considered, great and unexpected are the things perceived by those who are knights errant. For, what living person walking in through this castle door and seeing us here, would believe and judge us to be who we truly are?" Reality, as Don Quixote knows and Sancho has learned, is not what appearances show but what the keener, justice-informed eye perceives. And for this (Cervantes the writer implies, unconsciously undermining his military argument) letters are required.

"Historians," says Cervantes in Part I of *Don Quixote*,

"should be accurate, truthful and dispassionate, and neither interest nor fear, rancour nor affection should make them draw crooked the path of truth, whose mother is history, rival of time, safekeeper of events, witness of things past, example and caution of things present, warning of things to come." This paragraph is the example chosen by Jorge Luis Borges to show how different readers create through their readings different stories. In his famous fiction of 1939, "Pierre Menard, Author of *Don Quixote*," a "fake" biography written under the guise of a scholarly essay, Borges imagines a twentieth-century French writer, Pierre Menard, whose purpose is to write, once again, *Don Quixote*. Not to compose another *Quixote*, nor to transcribe or copy the original, but to create again, in a new time and place, word by word, the same novel as the one written by Cervantes. Borges then quotes the last section of the above paragraph, and compares Menard's version to that of the original; the words are, of course, the same. Cervantes's paragraph, however, according to Borges, is a mere rhetorical encomium of history. Menard's, instead, is an astonishing text: history, writes Menard, is the mother of truth. "Menard," says Borges, "a contemporary of William James, defines history not as an investigation of reality but as its source. Historical truth, for him, is not what took place; it is what we believe took place."

Borges's tongue-in-cheek distinction has a practical use. All reading is interpretation, every reading reveals and is dependent on the circumstances of its reader. And yet, if Cervantes's "reading" of his text betrays the conventions of his time, among those conventions is the notion (less astonishing to Cervantes's readers than to Menard's) that history is what we judge to be history, that reality is dictated not by tangible facts but by those that (in Coleridge's phrase) the reader's "suspension of disbelief" renders real. To repeat Alfred Döblin's observation: "It is not only the natural world that is constructed purposefully, but also events, history." The story that grants a society and each of its individuals an identity must, in order to serve its purpose of bringing a certain consciousness to our existence, not only shape itself throughout time upon what society legislates and considers proper, but also upon that which it considers alien and excludes. Perhaps in this way, by perceiving more keenly, it manages sometimes to circumvent Cassandra's curse and convince its readers that it serves something other than the ambitions of a Roman emperor or a Spanish archbishop.

The forgeries of the Sacromonte, reflected in the creation of *Don Quixote's* Arabic author, in turn reflected in the invented character of a knight errant who is really nothing but an old gentleman with a passion for adventure stories, are the fruits of a society that attempts to create for itself a forged identity. To deny its Arab and Jewish past, to wish for itself a Western purity of "untainted" blood and "immaculate" Christian faith, was for the Spain of Cervantes to admit that reality could be created out of illusions, erected like a stage set merely to oblige the ambitions and beliefs of those in power. Such an assumption, however, can never be exclusive: if one dreamworld is possible, then others, too, must be allowed for, and the invention of a Moorish Christian past, with its prophecies and holy relics, can be considered, in part at least, a corollary of the invention of an "uncontaminated" Christian present. Stories, as Don Quixote knew, grant a society its identity, but they cannot be just any story: they must respond to a shared reality which society itself fashions out of its myriad events, rooted in time and place, and yet fluid and everchanging. They can't be fictional inventions, in the sense of forgeries or misrepresentations; they need to be invented fictions, in the sense of discovering historical social truths that can be granted reality in narrative words. They must, in a deeply rooted literary sense, ring true.

V.

THE SCREEN OF HAL

"Time that is intolerant
Of the brave and innocent,
And indifferent in a week
To a beautiful physique,
Worships language and forgives
Everyone by whom it lives."

— W. H. Auden, "In Memory of W. B. Yeats"

WHEN WE SAY that we wish for a better, happier world, we usually mean better, happier for ourselves in particular. Somehow, the blame for our evils lies always with the neighbour, or the intruder, or the insider who went wrong, or with the enemy lurking outside the walls, the Barbarians eternally threatening to break in. Constantin Cavafy, in a famous poem, suggested that the day may come in which we are suddenly told that there are no Barbarians any longer. "Now what's going to happen to us without Barbarians?" Cavafy asked. "These people were a kind of solution."

The inimical other has long been "a kind of solution." To better guard us from him, we construct ever-more-perfected social mechanisms as protective devices erected to exclude the barbarian danger and that usually end by excluding most of us, excepting a happy few. These mechanisms have changed many times: from the earliest societies of hunter-gatherers to the vast multinational enterprises of today, from the democracy of the Greeks and the alliance network of the Incas to the serf system of feudalism and the Industrial Revolution of the nineteenth century, from the Roman and Chinese empires to the penitentiary regimes of Stalin and the Third Reich. For Aristotle, not possessing such a social structure, living outside the *polis* and not being subject to its *themites* — that is to say, existing outside the city-state built of stone and not subject to laws and customs written down in words — was itself the definition of a Barbarian.

These social structures function as political machineries, and also as economical, technological, and financial ones. They are both the internal and the external skeleton of our societies, allowed for by our laws and customs, and also the source of our laws and customs. They are all modelled on an ineffable ideal: the dream of a perfect social machine that will unerringly select what is good from what is bad, and eliminate the noxious while preserving only what is wholesome. That longed-for city blies always in the future. "For here we have no continuing city," wrote Saint Paul to the Hebrews, "but seek one to come." Philosophy and religion have endlessly attempted to define the workings of this city "to come," and on many occasions in our history its walls have seemed to lie almost within our reach, just beyond the horizon, and since the beginning of time stories have tried to tell us what such an ideal city might be like. "I look forward to a time when man shall progress upon something worthier and higher than his stomach," wrote the twenty-nine-year-old Jack London in 1905, "when there will be a finer incentive to impel men to action than the incentive of to-day, which is the incentive of the stomach. I retain my belief in the nobility and excellence of the human. I believe that spiritual sweetness and unselfishness will conquer the gross gluttony of to-day." To explain the workings of such a time, London, famous for his Klondike and South Sea fiction, imagined a number of fantastical plots in which both the worst and the best of what may happen is put forward in the shape of adventure stories.

The son of an itinerant astrologer who abandoned his family on the docks of San Francisco, Jack London grew up learning to thieve, drink, and box, and worked as a sailor, a laundry-boy, a coal-shifter in a power station, an oyster-pirate, and as unsuccessful goldigger in the Klondike, before discovering literature in the "Seaside Library," a series of popular fiction in which, he said, "with the exception of the villains and the adventuresses, all men and women thought beautiful thoughts, spoke a beautiful tongue, and performed glorious deeds." Soon London began writing himself, and became so successful that he ended up making more money from the capitalist press he so despised than any other writer in his time. He said that he had learned to tell a story while travelling as a bum across the States, when getting a hot meal or being chased from the doorstep depended on finding exactly the right pitch "the moment the housewife opened the door." At twenty, he read the *Communist Manifesto* and decided to join the Socialist Party, from which he resigned in 1916 "because of its lack of fire and fight, and its loss of emphasis on the class struggle." A few months later, on the night of November 21, 1916, in the luxurious California mansion that he had bought with his ever-growing royalties, Jack London decided to kill himself. Thinking that it would hasten the end, he took lethal doses of two different drugs. The effect was the opposite: the drugs worked against each other, and London lay in agony for more than twenty-four hours. He was forty years old.

Among London's unfinished writings was the manuscript of a novel, together with a number of notes for a possible ending. The novel bore the splendid title of *The Assassination Bureau, Ltd.*, a social machine so perfectly devised against the Barbarians that it cannot be stopped except by the destruction of its maker. The inventor is a certain Ivan Dragomiloff, who has set up a secret society that will, for a price, assassinate upon request. The Barbarians, however, the would-be victims, are not simply anyone a client might dislike. Once a name has been proposed for destruction, Dragomiloff conducts an investigation into the behaviour and character of the target. Only if, according to his judgement, the killing is "socially justifiable," does Dragomiloff give the order to act. A Barbarian is a Barbarian only if he is deemed so in Dragomiloff's eyes.

The Assassination Bureau is a perfectly honed machine. Once the request for an assassination has been put forward and the cash price has been paid, the client must wait for Dragomiloff's subordinates to offer the master proof of the would-be victim's misconduct. The victim may be a brutal chief of police, a ruthless impresario, a greedy banker, a labour grafter, an aristocratic *grande dame*: in every case, it must be demonstrated, beyond all doubt, that the person causes harm to society. If the proof is not sufficient, or if the victim dies accidentally, the money is returned to the client, less ten percent to cover the administrative costs. But once Dragomiloff has judged that the death is merited, there is no turning back. "An order once given," he himself explains, "is as good as accomplished. We cannot carry on our business otherwise. We have our rules, you know."

And then something unexpected occurs. In an attempt to dismantle the Bureau, an enterprising young man puts in a unique request for assassination. He meets with Dragomiloff and pays the price for the murder of an unnamed but very important public figure; only after Dragomiloff has accepted the request (on condition, of course, that the person be proven guilty), the young man reveals his victim's name: Dragomiloff himself. Since the Bureau never goes back on its word, Dragomiloff accepts the request for his own assassination. Dragomiloff has created a social machinery so efficient that its declared purpose, the elimination of socially undesirable characters upon request, overrides even the life of its own designer.

Jack London's story, from more than a century ago, in spite of suffering at times from the "beautiful tongue" of his "Seaside Library" readings, has today a curious contemporary ring. Not because of its suggestion that a bureau might be set up to eliminate those whom we deem to be society's pests (reminiscent of Gilbert and Sullivan's Lord High Executioner's "little list" of undesirables), but because of London's notion that a social machinery may be so perfected in its fanatical aim that it can only be destroyed by destroying its creators as well. At the risk of stretching a comparison a little too far, I believe that the Assassination Bureau has enjoyed a modern reincarnation. I believe that, in our time, we, too, have allowed for the construction of many such formidable social machineries that, like the Bureau itself, are multinational and anonymous, but whose purpose is not to purify society through assassination (no doubt a reprehensible goal), but to attain for a handful of individuals (among them, those whom Dragomiloff agrees to murder) the greatest possible financial profit, regardless of the cost to society and protected by a screen of countless anonymous shareholders. Unconcerned with the consequences, these machineries invade every area of human activity and look everywhere for monetary gain, even at the cost of human life: of everyone's life, since, in the end, even the richest and the most powerful will not survive the depletion of our planet.

Perhaps naively, London attempted to talk his way into the world of Dragomiloffs. "I met men," he said, "who invoked the name of the Prince of Peace in their diatribes against war, and who put rifles in the hands of [their private police] with which to shoot down strikers in their own factories. I met men incoherent with indignation at the brutality of prize-fighting, and who, at the same time, were parties to the adulteration of food that killed each year more babies than even red-handed Herod had killed. I talked in hotels and clubs and homes and Pullmans and steamer-chairs with captains of industry, and marveled at how little travelled they were in the realm of intellect. On the other hand, I discovered that their intellect, in the business sense, was abnormally developed. Also, I discovered that their morality, where business was concerned, was nil. This delicate, aristocratic-featured gentleman was a dummy director and a tool of corporations that secretly robbed widows and orphans. This gentleman, who collected fine editions and was an especial patron of literature, paid blackmail to a heavy-jowled, black-browed boss of a municipal machine. This editor, who published patent medicine advertisements and did not dare print the truth in his paper about said patent medicines for fear of losing the advertising, called me a scoundrelly demagogue because I told him that his political economy was antiquated and that his biology was contemporaneous with Pliny." With a few changes of style and a few up-to-date examples, London's diatribe is as valid today as it was in 1905. London's Dragomiloff conceived a social machine to kill upon request after payment of ready cash; we have set up economic machineries to make limitless amounts cash, no matter what the cost in lives. Both ultimately fail because, in their very perfection, they are doomed to destroy their makers.

The better, happier world longed for by London, in a society that had not yet known either of the World Wars, never came into being. But our stories keep searching for it, whether describing the worst or conceiving the best of all possible worlds, offering us over and over again scenarios that exist in the tension between these two extremes. For every reading of Don Quixote as a madman in a well-ordered society there will be one that sees him as the most rational of justice-seekers in a world that is both mad and unjust.

Language lends voice to the storytellers who try to tell us who we are; language builds out of words our reality and those who inhabit it, within and without the walls; language offers stories that lie and stories that tell the truth. Language changes with us, grows stronger or weaker with us, survives or dies with us. The economic machineries we have built require language to appeal to its consumers, but only on a dogmatic, practical level, deliberately avoiding literature's constant probing and interrogation. The endless sequence of readings of *Gilgamesh* or *Don Quixote* opens realms of meaning on countless subjects — personal identity, relationship to power, social duties and responsibilities, the balance of action — all of which may at some point entail a questioning of power and call for the resolution of injustice. To sustain the run of the machineries, those in office will often attempt to curb and control this multiplicity of readings in many ways: by simply prohibiting the book or, more subtly, by imposing a restricted or distorted vocabulary, by "blunting the language," as Günter Grass once called it. This censorship (because of course, it is censorship) takes place in many ways, from the most dramatic to the most covert. It may ban a language entirely, it may subvert certain vocabularies, it may distort or empty of meaning certain of words, it may channel language into limp literary productions or limit it to dogmatic use in the realms of politics, commerce, fashion, and, of course, religion. In every case, its aim is to prevent the telling and reading of true stories.

One of the most radical methods of this censorship consists in forbidding the use of languages other than the official one. The banning of Catalan or Basque during Franco's dictatorship, the attempt to suppress native languages in North America, the early laws in Canada against the use and teaching of French, the interdiction of Arabic in medieval Catholic Spain and in nineteenth-century French North Africa, were intended, on the one hand, to equate all languages with the language of those in power and, on the other hand, to denigrate the language of certain groups to the condition of Barbarian: less efficient, less intelligent, less civilized. In the eye of the censor, whoever speaks that other language is identified with something "lesser." The prejudice is ancient: according to Pliny, the strange languages spoken by many of the fabulous races he described led him to conclude that, because they seemed to grunt and squeal instead of speaking, "foreigners" were "hardly members of the human species." Pliny's dictum, explicitly or implicitly, rings throughout our many bloody centuries: the language spoken by "foreigners" often brands them as "hardly a member of the human species" and therefore justifies, in the view of the ruling class, a different treatment.

Not only through censorship of whole languages do totalitarian governments enforce restrictions on thought: by using certain words in specific contexts and by making up words to denote assumed rights and privileges, the impression can be created that what is being said in this new vocabulary is intrinsically true simply because words exist to say it: the words *democratic*, *freedom of speech*, *equality*, *liberal* are all good examples. Another is the term *human rights*, as used during the military dictatorship in Argentina. In Spanish, "human rights" translates as "*derechos humanos*" but the word *derecho* means both "right" and "upright." In the mid-1970s, Amnesty International publicly denounced the military government's violation of human rights. In response, a right-wing popular magazine supplied its readers with postcards of protest to send to the organization. The postcard read: "*Nosotros argentinos somos derechos y humanos*," "We Argentinians are upright and human."

Distortions of this kind are, of course, the essence of demagogical and of commercial language, intent on "selling" an idea or product upon whose "truth" we are meant *not* to reflect. In 1907, Jack London and his friend

Arthur George mocked an attempt within the Socialist Movement to create a simplified language for the use of the proletariat. London and George suggested, tongue-in-cheek, that, in keeping with this Socialist aim, a number of "difficult" words "be as rapidly as possible retired to academic obscurity, or entirely abolished" from the English language, in order to replace "the anarchistic language and ideals that now prevail." The list of three hundred words included Adultery, Aristocracy, Brothel, Capitalist, Dictator, Oligarchy and Working-Class.

In most cases, of course, the changes imposed by force upon language are effected much more subtly and gradually, through the deliberately erroneous use of certain words stripped of their radical meaning, and also through the artifice of jinglelike catchphrases, the clever use of puns and malicious *double entendre*. In this way, literary language (ambiguous, open, complex, infinitely capable of enrichment) can be supplanted by that of advertising (short, categorical, imperious, final,) so that eventually answers are offered instead of questions, and instant and superficial gratification takes the place of difficulty and depth.

Not only commercial slogans and official discourse derive from this distorted use of language. A kind of literature, too, can be created from this emasculated vocabulary, and it is easy for readers and writers to be seduced into its comfortable aesthetics and wit. Though the intrinsic effect of such work is political, its ostensible purpose is to be purely entertaining, a "cultural product" as it began to be called in the twentieth century. The state

of the book industry today is symptomatic of the effects
of these subtler forms of censorship.

The economic model applied since the Industrial Revolution to most technologies and most forms of
commerce, to produce goods at the lowest possible cost
for the highest possible profit, reached in the 1900s the
realm of the book. To achieve this goal, the greater part of
the book industry, especially in the Anglo-Saxon world,
developed a team of specialists charged with determining
which books would be produced based on a supposedly
mathematical forecast of which books would sell. From
the strategist of editorial marketing departments to the
buyer for the larger bookstore chains and also, perhaps
less consciously aware of their responsibility, editors and
creative-writing teachers, almost every member of the
book industry became, to a large extent, part of a production line for the creation of artifacts for an audience not of
readers (in the traditional sense) but of consumers. Certainly, many who were moved by a love of books to enter
the industry remain stubbornly faithful to that calling,
but they do so in spite of strong pressure, especially
within the larger publishing groups, to consider the book
above all as a saleable object. Though there are, of course,
publishers who have succeeded in retaining their literary
integrity, more and more publishing decisions are
deferred to marketing departments and to the buyers for
chain bookshops, and, as a consequence, critical self-
censorship and commercial considerations creep with
increasing frequency into the editorial realm.

The strategies of the industry are blatant and self-referential. In the film version of *The Devil Wears Prada*, based on one of these books produced on a specific model (the model known as "chick lit") and marketed accordingly, the main evil character, the fashion mogul Miranda Priestly, says to the innocent heroine who refuses to bend to the "fashion mentality," that the colour of the dress she's wearing, bought no doubt at an ordinary supermarket, is the result of careful fashion planning a season earlier; that is to say, that the dictates of commercial dogma are made to impregnate so deeply the fabric of society that no strand remains unaffected, and even though we might consciously refuse to follow the day's fashion, we will nevertheless become "slaves to the system."

This is a self-fulfilling truth. The book industry not only produces this dogma, but also makes sure that very little place is accorded to anything outside it. Bookstore chains sell their window space and display tables to the highest bidder, so that what the public sees is what the publisher pays for. In consequence, piles of announced best-sellers occupy most of the physical space available in a bookstore, all carrying an implicit "sell-by" date, like eggs, that ensures a continuous production. Book supplements, forced by a general newspaper policy of addressing supposedly low-brow readers, accord more and more space to those same "fast-food" books, thereby creating the impression that "fast-food" books are as worthy as any old-fashioned classic, or that the readers are not intelligent enough to enjoy "good" literature. This last point is all important: the industry must educate us in our stupidity, because we don't come by stupidity naturally. On the contrary, we come into the world as intelligent creatures, curious and avid for instruction. It takes immense time and effort, individually and collectively, to dull and eventually stifle our intellectual and aesthetic capabilities, our creative perception, and our use of language.

Paradoxically, it is the very rich nature of language that allows for it to be co-opted, to be reduced to dogma or, on the contrary, to flourish as literature. The perceived communality of language, its implied share of meanings, the cumulative effects created by successive interpretations, render a text susceptible to rulings of many kinds. Any great book incorporates into its pages all previous readings, so that, after a first incursion, *Dr. Jekyll and Mr. Hyde* disarms its own surprise ending, assimilates its conclusion into its beginning, rewrites itself in the reader's mind with a mass of comments and glosses that have sprung up since its first publication, so that we can no longer read Stevenson's *Dr. Jekyll and Mr. Hyde* but the *Dr. Jekyll and Mr. Hyde* as read by the Victorians, by its pre- and post-Freudian audience, by modernists and postmodernists, and so on into the future. The only way to stop this geometrically progressive reading would be to freeze the text in one single authoritarian moment, declaring, as if it were God's word, on pain of some terrible punishment, that no variations will be allowed. But instead of promoting books of breadth and depth, for the most part the publishing industry of our time creates one-dimensional objects, books that are surface only and that don't allow readers the possibility of exploration.

Obviously there are countless writers who refuse to work according to formulae, and some who succeed in doing so, but much of what is being produced by the larger publishing companies today follows the set industrial model. A large portion of the reading public is therefore trained to expect a certain kind of "comfortable" book and, what is far more noxious, to read in a certain "comfortable" way, looking for short descriptions, patterns of dialogue copied from television sitcoms, familiar brand names, and plots that may follow convoluted entanglements but never allow for complexity or ambiguity.

The German philosopher Axel Honneth, using a term coined by Georg Lukács, calls this process *reification*. By reification, Lukács meant the colonization of the world of experience by means of one-dimensional generalisations derived from the rules of commercial exchange: granting value and identity not through imaginative stories but merely according to what something is said to cost and how much someone is willing to pay for it. This commercial fetishism covers all fields of human activity, including consciousness itself, and lends human labour and industrial commodities a sort of illusory autonomy, so that we become their subservient onlookers. Honneth extended this concept to embrace our conceptions of the other, of the world, and of ourselves, that is to say, a view of society that sees humans and their realm not as living entities but as things or quantities lacking singular identities. For Honneth, the most serious of these concepts is that of "auto-reification," exemplified in the way we present ourselves to others in activities as diverse as job interviews, company-training programs, virtual-sex chat-sites on the Web, and role-playing video games. I would add to these the passive reading habits that deny our own intelligence and make us accept that the only stories we deserve are those pre-digested for us.

In the world of the book, this process of reification takes place by means of an industrial manipulation known as the editing process. Implanted in all English-language publishing companies since the early twentieth century, and uncommon in all other languages (though the system is filtering in because of the influence of the English market throughout the world), the industrialized editing process is built upon several fallacies denounced in Honneth's argument. Among them, the most danger-ous one assumes that a literary text is "perfectible": that is to say, that writing must aspire to a kind of Platonic archetype, an ideal model of literary text. It follows then that this ideal can be attained with the help of a specialist, an editor acting as tuner or mechanic who can "perfect" the text through professional reading skills. A literary creation is thus considered not an intrinsic "work-in-progress," never closed, never definitive, arrested at the moment of publication ("We publish to stop revising," declared the Mexican writer Alfonso Reyes), but as a more or less all-rounded product initiated by the writer, finished off by an editor, and approved by various spe-cialists in marketing and sales. Anthony Burgess, in a review of D. H. Lawrence's *Sons and Lovers*, complained about this editing procedure: "I think that the Anglo-

American publishing tradition needs, at this point, to be taken to task. The editor who lacks the creative gift but is compensated with artistic taste has been overmuch lauded. Some of us would like to know what Thomas Wolfe wrote before Maxwell Perkins got hold of him, or what *Catch-22* was like before the editorial finesse of the former editor of *The New Yorker* licked it into shape. Editors never emend orchestral scores or panoramic paintings; why should the novelist be singled out as the one artist who doesn't understand his art?"

Of course, every writer has his or her homegrown editor: a spouse, a friend, or even a professional editor may have acquired, over time, the writer's trust as someone whose opinion the writer can measure, and choose to follow or set aside. And a fair number of professional editors, in the midst of ever-increasing constraints, courageously continue to try to work in service of the writer, not the industry, helping the author understand the work more clearly and achieve a book with fewer failings. I myself have been blessed with two or three such editors, one in particular whom I thanked in a dedication some time ago for having taught me to write; it would be unconscionable of me not to state publicly how much I owe to her intelligence, intellectual rigour, and personal taste. The work of such editors seems even more remarkable when we consider that they battle against the demands of the large industrial conglomerates to produce industrially efficient, quick-selling literature that equates difficulty with lack of skill, demands resolutions to each fictional situation and affirmations to every imaginative doubt, presents a fully understandable image of the world from which all complexities have been eliminated and for which no new learning is required, offering in its place a state of mindless "happiness."

This literature exists in every genre, from sentimental fiction to the bloodthirsty thriller, from the historical romance to mystical claptrap, from true confessions to the realistic drama. It confines "saleable" literature firmly to the realm of entertainment, of relaxation, of pastime, and therefore of that which is socially superfluous and ultimately unessential. It infantilizes both writers and readers by making the former believe that their creations must be licked into shape by someone who knows better, and by convincing the latter that they are not clever enough to read more intelligent and complex narrations. In the book industry today, the larger the targeted audience, the more obediently the writer is expected to follow the instructions of editors and booksellers (and lately of literary agents as well), allowing them to decree not only practical copyediting changes of fact and grammar, but also of plot, character, setting, and title. In the meantime, books that were earlier considered not abstruse and academic but merely intelligent are published now mainly by university presses and small companies with heroic budgets. The controller in Aldous Huxley's 1932 novel *Brave New World* explains these tactics succinctly: "that's the price we have to pay for stability. You've got to choose between happiness and what people used to call high art. We've sacrificed the high art."

The Dutch doctor Bernard de Mandeville, who set up

his practice in England in the early eighteenth century, published in 1714 an essay he called *The Fable of the Bees, or Private Vices, Public Benefits*, in which he argued that the system of mutual assistance which allows society, like a beehive, to function, feeds on the honeyed passion of consumers who love to acquire what they don't need. A virtuous society, Mandeville maintained, in which only the basic requirements must be satisfied, would have neither trade nor culture, and therefore collapse for want of employment. The consumer society that came fully into being almost two centuries later, took Mandeville's sarcastic arguments literally. Flattering the senses, valuing possession over worth or need, it turned the notion of value on its head: value, according to the codes of advertising, became not the worth of an object nor a service measured in its practice, but a perception based on how extensively the service or object was promoted and under what brand name. In the consumer world, Berkeley's *esse est percepi* has a different meaning. Perception is at the root of being, but things acquire value not because they need to exist but because they are perceived as being needed. Desire becomes then not the source but the end-product of consumption.

To achieve this state of desire, advertising proceeds according to literary patterns. The story with which the consumer is made to identify, follows, in most cases, the model of what George Eliot, in 1856, defined as "silly novels," "determined," she wrote, "by the particular quality of silliness that predominates in them — the frothy, the prosy, the pious, or the pedantic." These stories boast a "driveling kind of dialogue, and equally driveling narrative, which, like a bad drawing, represents nothing, and barely indicates what is meant to be represented."

Like the language of best-selling "silly novels," the "happy language" of consumerism, of publicity, and of political slogans is employed to communicate short, simple messages representing nothing, aimed at convincing, never at opening an exchange, never at allowing in-depth exploration. "Drink Coca-Cola," like "Argentinians are upright and human," cannot be read deeply without destruction; these statements bear no argument except that of their own commands. The language of advertising, honed and perfected in the United States in the early twentieth century in order to sell everything to everyone and, above all, boasting the virtues of the quick and easy, is a language that equates simplicity with truth. Rather than stories, it tells summaries of stories, desiccated to the point that its moral will always be one that satisfies our most egotistical desires.

For Jack London, writers were supposed to write critically: that is to say, the vision they gave of reality was always once removed, not only because it had been filtered through the screen of words, but especially because the only objectivity possible was a subjective one, derived from a tone that often, very often, slipped into irony in order "to better tell the truth." Almost a century later, in 1993, David Foster Wallace, the author of the celebrated and very long novel, *Infinite Jest*, in an article entitled *"E Pluribus Unum,"* argued that the American writers of the previous generation (DeLillo, Gaddis, Pynchon) had enfeebled the confidence of his contemporaries by using this sustained ironic tone in their stories about America. Wallace suggested that a change in the writer's viewpoint might be called for, and that instead of chronicling the reality of American society from a position of intellectual superiority, it would be wise to try to understand instead the "beauty and wisdom" of that which this culture offered daily. "Fiction writers as a species," said Wallace, "tend to be ogglers. They tend to lurk and to stare. They are born watchers. They are viewers." But because the older generation watched through the glasses of "irony and ridicule," though "entertaining and effective," they were at the same time "agents of a great despair and stasis in U.S. culture." For aspiring fiction writers, Wallace said, they posed especially terrible problems. According to Wallace, not the reality but the critical treatment of that reality threatened his own creative capabilities. "Irony tyrannizes us," he warned. What Wallace proposed was a revisionist perspective of the culture created by American consumer society, thereby lending intellectual credibility to the tenets of advertising. "The new rebels," says Wallace, no doubt including himself, "might be artists willing to risk the yawn, the rolled eyes, the cool smile, the nudged ribs, the parody of gifted ironists, the 'Oh how *banal.*'" Unwittingly ironic, Wallace proposes not to ironize about mercantile America but to find a new aesthetic for it, to be creative with its creations, to accept "reification" as a laudable state of being.

In his essential diary of the Nazi years, *I Will Bear Witness*, the linguist Victor Klemperer, noted that it was precisely the tactics of American advertising that the Nazis copied for their propaganda, distorting them for their own purpose. The language of advertising in the United States was merely naive; that of Nazi Germany was lethal. "The superlativism," wrote Klemperer on January 18, 1938, "which is a special hallmark of the language of the Third Reich, is different from the American one. The people in the USA talk big in a childlike and fresh manner, the Nazis do it in a way that is half megalomania, half frantic autosuggestion." Four years earlier, Klemperer had already noted this use of advertising language in a speech by Goebbels: "We practice an 'active influencing' of the people," Goebbels had explained to a crowd, "complemented by a systematic long-term education of a people." According to Goebbels, propaganda "must not lie," it must "be creative." Not, of course, in the sense of lending a self-revealing identity to the reader, but rather inventing a false and brittle mask that hides and does not reveal.

This creative function of advertising (that of altering reality by transforming literary language into dogma) is clearly evident in religious propaganda. The subject is so vast and complex that I will only mention it here to say that, like political and commercial propaganda, religious propaganda employs a language of its own which, as in any kind of advertising, must be stripped of depth and ambiguity, must become dogmatic in order to be meaningful, must in fact submit to "reification." Religious propaganda aims at a form of consumption: not of commodities but of ideas, or rather of adamant precepts that must be acquired by the "believer-consumer" (the term is

Honneth's) not out of need but out the illusion of need. Proclamations, gestures, articles of clothing, talismans, et cetera, become, through this propaganda, not symbolic of a belief but the demonstration of the belief itself.

All these forms of advertising (in the realms of politics, publishing, and religion) illustrate the transformation of creative language into one fit only for commerce, a transformation that in the process effectively destroys literature's illuminating powers. Literature is the opposite of dogma. A literary text lies constantly open to other readings, to other interpretations, perhaps because literature, unlike dogma, allows both for freedom of thought and for freedom of expression, and is, like those essential genes that granted us the power of imagination, self-reproductive. I find it moving that no literary text is utterly original, no literary text is completely unique, that it stems from previous texts, built on quotations and misquotations, on the vocabularies fashioned by others and transformed through imagination and use. Writers must find consolation in the fact that there is no very first story and no very last one. Our literature reaches further back than the beginnings our memory permits us, and further into the future than our imagination allows us to conceive, but that must be the only barrier. "Freedom of expression," declared the Egyptian theologian Gamal Al-Banna, commenting on recent manifestations of Islamic extremism, "is an integral part of the freedom of thought. I believe that all opinions must be accepted. Otherwise, there is no freedom. Freedom can find its own limits, but to impose them from outside is contrary to its nature and risks destroying it." Such freedom requires the use of literary language, the same that our industrial machineries attempt to exclude.

A similar pattern of cultural impoverishment as the one we are experiencing today, occurred centuries earlier, with the decline of Latin in the early Middle Ages. The extent of the Roman Empire had brought Latin to regions as far as the Middle East, the Spanish Peninsula to the west, the British Isles to the north, and Mediterranean Africa to the south. But with Rome no longer at its centre, universal Latin became enfeebled in both its semantics and its grammar, ineffectual as an instrument of both conversation and storytelling. The historian Erich Auerbach described its scope as limited to "an over-all provincialism, a narrowness of horizon, a preoccupation with local problems, interests, and traditions," and while a certain number of authors developed a style "mannered to the point of absurdity," most of the writing in Latin became "unadorned, utilitarian prose tending towards colloquial speech in its sentence structure, tone, and choice of words." Lacking stories.

Stories tell us that our better, happier world lies always just beyond our reach, in another time and place, in a long-lost past, in the fabulous Golden Age longed for by Don Quixote, or in the future, on a distant planet or a contented Earth. In Stanley Kubrick's film, *2001: A Space Odyssey*, scripted by Arthur C. Clarke and Kubrick himself, the world we try to reach is on Jupiter. To achieve this goal, a spaceship has been built, controlled by a supercomputer, HAL 9000, known to the five members of the crew simply as Hal. Hal has been programmed to steer the ship to its destination, with the specific instruction to eliminate whatever obstacles it may encounter. An artificial intelligence machine, Hal (in the voice of Canadian actor Douglas Rain) is capable of speaking and interacting like a human being, and can even simulate human emotion. Unlike humans, however, Hal is supposedly incapable of error.

After some time, Hal announces that something is wrong in the ship's communications system. One of the crew, Bowman, exits to repair the fault but can't find one; back on Earth, the controllers conclude that Hal must be mistaken. Bowman and another member decide to disconnect the computer to avoid further problems, but in spite of their precautions, Hal discovers their plan and proceeds to eliminate Bowman's partner and to cut off the oxygen supply of four of the crew members. Bowman, left alone to outwit the computer, realizes that Hal's "mistake" was, in fact, deliberate. Instructed to have the ship reach its destination "at all costs," Hal concluded that the greatest obstacle to the mission's goal was the fallibility of human intelligence and, since the programmers did not include in his "mind" the prohibition of killing the crew, Hal logically decided to eliminate the source of all possible errors: human beings themselves.

Like Jack London's Assassination Bureau, Hal is a failproof machine, built to reach the wished-for goal "at all costs," even at the cost of its maker's life. The mercantile structure that we have built as the driving engine of our society is as perfect as those other imaginary constructs, and as lethal. We have given it the command to reach a goal, to render financial profit at all cost; we have forgotten to inscribe in its memory the *caveat*: except at the cost of our lives. For the vast economic machinery that governs every aspect of our societies, as well as for the all-judging Dragomiloff or the technologically perfect Hal, we are the Barbarians. That appears to be the identity awaiting us.

In our search for structures within which we can be with one another, we may have ended up with societies from whose benefits we all seem destined to be excluded. Disregarding the abuse of human rights for the sake of economic partnerships, allowing the devastation of the planet with the excuse of ever-increasing financial benefits, refusing to adopt scientific solutions because of superstitious beliefs: all these things allow such partnerships, profits, and beliefs to overide the responsibilities we have toward each other, toward ourselves individually, and toward the world.

In the *Epic of Gilgamesh*, it becomes clear that the unjust king and the wild man can learn from each other, and that the laws of that society must allow it to profit from the learning of both. But these laws not only prescribe that the king must be just and the wild man become civilized; they also set limits to the land that the city may occupy, and to how far its dominion may extend, and to the length and breadth of its walls, as the city defines and redefines itself throughout its changing history. This shifting identity is the subject of our best stories, recalling the experience of our past and imagining a better life as a model for the present; but it can also, at times, try to impose fake stories for our consumption, whether to justify a position of power or to bleed the power from our readings.

We live in a world of fluid borders and identities. The slow movements of migration and conquest that defined the shape of the earth for thousands of years have, in the past few decades, accelerated a hundredfold so that, as in a fast-forwarded film, nothing and no one seems to remain fixed in one place for long. Attached to a certain site through birth, blood-ties, learned affection or acquired need, we relinquish or are forced to relinquish these attachments and shift into new allegiances and devotions that in turn will shift again, sometimes backward, sometimes forward, away from an imagined centre. These movements cause anxiety, individually and socially. Individually, because our identity changes with the displacement. We leave our home forcibly or through choice, as exiles and refugees or as immigrants or travellers, threatened or persecuted in our homeland or merely attracted by other landscapes and other civilizations. Socially, because if we stay, the place we call home changes. The arrival of new cultures, the ravages of war and of industrial upheavals, the shifts of political divisions and ethnic regroupings, the strategies of multinational companies and global trade, make it almost impossible to hold for long on to a shared definition of nationality. The terrible question that the Caterpillar asks Alice in Wonderland has always been difficult to answer; today, in our kaleidoscopic universe, it has become so precarious as to be almost meaningless: "Who are *You*?"

Gerald Manley Hopkins, writing in 1876, recognized the essence of our human condition in this ambiguous state of permanence and transience:

> I am soft sift
> In an hourglass — at the wall
> Fast, but mined with a motion, a drift . . .

Fast is the key word of our existence, in both its contradictory meanings. We hold fast to a social identity that we believe lends us a name and a face, but equally fast we move from one definition of society to another, altering again and again that presumed identity. Like characters in a story that keeps changing, we find ourselves playing roles that others appear to have invented for us, in plots whose roots and consequences escape us. We declare ourselves Roman or Carthaginian, but our notion of what Rome and Carthage are is either too restricted or too ambitious to be useful beyond the shorthand of a label. Vague and heated patriotic feelings, murky reasons of emotion and faith, lead us to defend or attack a border or a banner whose shape and colour keep shifting, and even when declaring allegiance to one place, we seem to be always moving away from it, toward a nostalgic image of what we believe that place once was or might one day be. Nationalities, ethnicities, tribal, and religious filiations imply geographical and political definitions of some kind, and yet, partly because of our nomad nature and partly due the fluctuations of history, our geography is less grounded in a physical than in a phantom landscape. Home is always an imaginary place.

This may seem an odd affirmation at a time when, after the dissolution of most of the imperial powers, nationalism, both political and religious, seems more virulent than almost ever before. The separatist voices, each claiming superiority and self-sufficiency, have become increasingly louder, and in many cases allow for such extreme violence that even self-destruction, according to their arguments, is justified to kill the Philistines. Two mottoes define the vast majority of these movements. The first, coined by the Chilean independentists of the nineteenth century, still appears on Chile's coat-of-arms: "By Reason or By Force." The second is that of the nationalists who founded the Irish Republic in 1919: *Sin Fein*, "Ourselves Alone."

Beyond the will to impose one-sided laws and to claim privileges for a perceived singularity, it is difficult to understand what we mean when we speak today of a national identity. Outside local colour and racist caricature, and independent of circumstantial questions of political economy and industrial strategies, how do we define the society to which we say we belong and which in turn defines us? What is this hourglass within which we shift and whose shape and nature keep changing? By what means do we imagine ourselves in a place we call home? And who are we, its inhabitants, settled in or moving through?

Answers of some sort, or rather, better-phrased questions, can be found in certain stories, such as the ones I've mentioned throughout these talks. And yet stories, even the best and truest, can't save us from our own folly. Stories can't protect us from suffering and error, from natural and artificial catastrophes, from our own suicidal greed. The only thing they can do is sometimes, for reasons impossible to foresee, they can tell us of that folly and that greed, and remind us to be vigilant of our increasingly perfected technologies. Stories can offer consolation for suffering and words to name our experience. Stories can tell us who we are and what are these hourglasses through which we sift, and suggest ways of imagining a future that, without calling for comfortable happy endings, may offer us ways of remaining alive, together, on this much-abused earth.

ACKNOWLEDGEMENTS

EVERY BOOK IS a collaboration. Among the friends and colleagues who have helped me in writing this one, I would like to thank Bernie Lucht for the confidence first shown to me a quarter of a century ago, when Damiano Pietropaolo invited this Canadian newcomer to do a series for CBC's *Ideas*; John Fraser for suggesting my name to the Massey Lectures committee; Lucie Pabel and Gottwalt Pankow for their illuminating comments; Susan Middleton for lending a sympathetic ear to an early draft; Doris Lessing for certain ideas about the role of the writer in our society; Roberto Calasso for his reinterpretation of Kafka's aphorisms; Philip Coulter of CBC and Lynn Henry of House of Anansi Press for their generous reading, as well as for suggesting a better title for these lectures; Heather Sangster for the careful copyediting, and Bill Douglas for the elegant design; Professor Isaias Lerner for his literature classes, far away and long ago;

Professor Manuel Barrios Aguilera for a private lesson on the *libros plúmbeos* in Granada; Stan Persky for a conversation on Christa Wolf's *Cassandra*; Guillermo Schavelzon, Claude Roquet, and Sylviane Sambord for several discussions on the fate of the printed word; Graeme Gibson and Margaret Atwood for sharing their enthusiasm for Inuit storytelling; the Centre national du livre in France for its support; Bruce Westwood and his team for their kind assistance.

My thanks, above all, to Craig Stephenson, whose care, intelligence, and love makes everything seem possible.

NOTES

1. The Voice of Cassandra

Three books proved immensely helpful as preparation for this chapter: Philippe Descola's *Par-delà nature et culture* (Gallimard: Paris, 2005); Peter Berger and Thomas Luckmann's *The Social Construction of Reality: A Treatise in the Sociology of Knowledge* (Pelican Books: Harmondsworth, Middlesex, 1984) and André Béteille, *Anti-Utopia: Essential Writings of A.B.*, edited with an Introduction by Dipankar Gupta (Oxford University Press: Oxford & London, 2005). A second reading of Karl R. Popper's classic *The Open Society and Its Enemies* (Harper & Row: New York, 1962) proved as disturbing as when I first came across it almost forty years ago.

The quotations from Alfred Döblin are taken from various sources. The letter to T. F. Marinetti is quoted in the introduction by Brigitte Vergne-Cain and Gérard Rudent to Alfred Döblin, *Die Ermordung einer Butterblume und andere Erzählungen* (Le Livre de Poche: Paris, 1990).

I read Döblin's "Der Bau des epischen Werks" (first published in *Jahrbuch der Sektion für Dichtkunst*, Berlin, 1929) in *Schriften zur Asthetik, Poetik und Literatur*, edited by Erich Kleinschmidt (Olten and Freiburg i. Br., 1989) and Döblin's *Schicksalsreise* (1949) in the English translation by Edna McCown, published as *Destiny's Journey: Flight From the Nazis*, with an introduction by Peter Demetz (Paragon House: New York, 1992). The edition I used of Döblin's *Berlin Alexanderplatz: Die Geschichte vom Franz Biberkopf* is that of Walter Muschg (Deutscher Taschenbuch Verlag: München, 1965). Several of Döblin's notions on the social role of the artist I took from his collection of short pieces, *Flucht und Sammlung des Judenvolks* (Gerstenberg Verlag: Hildeseim, 1977).

The line by Eric Ormsby is from his essay "Poetry as Isotope: The Hidden Life of Words" in the splendid collection *Facsimiles of Time: Essays on Poetry and Translation* (The Porcupine's Quill: Erin, Ontario, 2001). Julian Jaynes, *The Origin of Consciousness in the Breakdown of the Bicameral Mind* (Princeton University Press: Princeton, 1976) continues to be for me an important reference. For the Jewish legends I've used two masterworks: Martin Buber's *Tales of the Hasidim* (Schocken Books: New York, 1947) and Louis Ginzberg's *The Legends of the Jews*, specifically the section on "Adam" in volume I: *From the Creation to Jacob*, translated by Henrietta Szold (Johns Hopkins University Press: Baltimore & London, 1998). The Robert F. Burton quotation is from his *Indica* (Memorial Edition, Tylston and Edwards: London, 1887), but I also consulted the English translation by W.D.P. Hill of Tulsi Das's *The Holy Lake of the Acts of Rama* (London, 1952). The story of Milena's friend appears in Margarete Buber-Neumann's *Kafkas Freundin Milena* (Georg Müller: Munich, 1968). Rubén Darío's poem, "Canto IX," is part of *Cantos de vida y esperanza* [1905] collected in *Poesías Completas*, edited by Luis Alberto Ruiz (Ediciones Antonio Zamora: Buenos Aires, 1967). I've used Paul Shorey's translation of Plato's "The Republic," in *The Collected Dialogues, Including the Letters*, edited by Edith Hamilton and Huntington Cairns (Bollingen Series, Princeton University Press: Princeton, N.J., 1961) and Ted Hughes's version of Aeschylus's "Agamemnon" in *The Oresteia*, (Faber & Faber: London, 1999). Jorge Luis Borges's story "El informe de Brodie" was first published in the collection of that name, (Emecé: Buenos Aires, 1970).

2. *The Tablets of Gilgamesh*

I found the following books useful as background for this chapter: Tzuetan Todorov's *Nous et les autres: La réflexion française sur la diversité humaine* (Editions du Seuil: Paris, 2004), René Girard's *La violence et le sacré* (Bernard Grasset: Paris, 1972), Slavoj Zizek, *Violencia en el acto: Conferencias de Buenos Aires*, compiled by Analía Hounie and translated into Spanish by Patricia Wilson (Paidós: Buenos Aires, Barcelona y México, 2004) and Israel Rosenfeld's *The Strange, Familiar and Forgotten: An Anatomy of Consciousness* (Alfred A. Knopf: New York, 1992)

George Smith's story of his discovery appears in his book *The Chaldean Account of Genesis* (Sampson Low, Marston, Searle & Rivington: London, 1846). I have used Stephen Mitchell's translation of *Gilgamesh* (Profile Books: London, 2004) but have also consulted those of Herbert Mason (Houghton Mifflin: New York, 1970), Derrek Hines (Chatto & Windus: London, 2002), and Jean Bottéro (*L'épopée de Gilgames: Le grand homme qui ne voulait pas mourir* (Gallimard: Paris,1992). Much of the information on Mesopotamia came from Bottéro's

Mésopotamie: L'écriture, la raison et les dieux (Gallimard: Paris, 1987). References to the double appear in E. T. A. Hoffmann, *Die Elixiere des Teufels* in *Gesammelte Werke in Einzelausgaben*, II Band (Aufbau-Verlag: Berlin & Weimar, 1982), Heinrich Heine, "Deutschland: ein Wintermärchen" in *Sämtliche Werke*, II Band, herausgegeben von Prof. Dr. Ernst Elster (Bibliographisches Institut: Leipzig & Wien, 1890), Edgar Allan Poe, "William Wilson" in *Tales of the Grotesque and Arabesque* in *The Works of Edgar Allan Poe*, volume II, edited by Edmund Clarence Stedman and George Edward Woodberry (Charles Scribner's Sons: New York, 1914). The quotations by Rudyard Kipling are from his poems "The British Flag" and "Recessional" in *The Definitive Edition of Rudyard Kipling's Verse* (Hodder & Stoughton: London etc., 1973), while Mr. Podsnap appears in Charles Dickens's *Our Mutual Friend* (2 vols., Society for English and French Literature: New York, n/d). Other quotations are taken from Strabo, *The Geography*, Book I, ch. 4, par. 9, translated by H. L. Jones (Heinemann: London, 1960); Robert Louis Stevenson, *The Strange Case of Dr. Jekyll and Mr. Hyde* in *The Works of R. L. Stevenson*, volume III (Thomas Nelson & Sons: New York, 1915); Nicholas Rankin, *Dead Man's Chest: Travels After Robert Louis Stevenson* (Faber & Faber: London & Boston, 1987); Oscar Wilde, *The Picture of Dorian Gray* in *The Works of Oscar Wilde*, edited with an Introduction by G. F. Maine (Collins: London & Glasgow, 1948); Hobbes, *Leviathan*, Part I, ch. 13 [1651] (Penguin Books: London etc., 1982).

Gordon Brown is quoted from Philip Johnston's piece, "Brown's Manifesto for Britishness," in *The Telegraph*, London, January 30, 2007. David Gordon White's *Myths of the Dog-Man*, with a foreword by Wendy Doniger (University of Chicago Press: Chicago and London, 1991) is essential reading on the subject of the other. The legend of Noah cursing his son Ham with the words "Damned be Canaan, may God make your face black!" appears for the first time in Arabic translations of a fourth-century commentary of Genesis attributed to St. Ephrem of Nisibis. The passage appears only in the translated versions, not in the original. Later historians, such as Ibn Khaldun in the fourteenth century, rejected the story as untrue. Cf. Ibn Khaldun, *Al-Muqaddima (Discours sur l'Histoire universelle) Traduit de l'arabe, présenté et annoté par Vincent Monteil* (Sindbad/Actes Sud: Paris, 1968). The quotation by St. Augustine is from *The City of God against the Pagans*, Part II, Book XVI, Chapter 8, a new translation by Henry Bettenson, with an Introduction by John O'Meara (Penguin Books: London and New York, 1984); the Arab terms for Westerners are mentioned in Ibn Khaldun, *Al-Muqaddima*. The lines from the *Chronicle of King Het'un* (Kirakos of Gandsak), the *Liang shu*, the *T'oung Pao*, etc. are quoted in Wendy Doniger O'Flaherty's *The Origins of Evil in Hindu Mithology* (University of California Press: Berkeley, CA, 1976). The reference to Jewish mythology is taken once again from Louis Ginzberg, *The Legends of the Jews*, Volume I (Johns Hopkins University Press: Baltimore, Md, 1998). The lines by Oliver Goldsmith are from his essay "National Prejudices" in *Essays and Criticisms by Dr. Goldsmith* (J. Johnson: London, 1798), though Morris Golden (in Modern Language Notes, Vol. 74, No. 1, January 1959) argues that this particular essay is not by Goldsmith.

The warnings to young Muslims travelling West come from Hamza Al-Mizeini's article "Don't Get Lost in the West, My Son" in *Al-Watan*, Abba, Saudi Arabia, March 2007.

3. The Bricks of Babel

The quotations in this chapter are from the King James Bible; from Franz Kafka's "Aphorismen" in *Beim Bau der chinesischen Mauer. und andere Schriften aus dem Nachlaß*, Band 6 in *Gesammelte Werke in zwölf Bänden* (Fischer Taschenbuch Verlag: Frankfurt am Main, 2002); from Thomas Carlyle's *Journal*, November 11, 1849; from James Boswell's *Life of Dr Johnson*, October 12, 1779 (Dent: London, 1973); Søren Kirkegaard, *Diapsalmata*, [deuxième texte de la première partie de *L'Alternative*, 1843] traduit du danois par Paul-Henri Tisseau, revu par Else-Marie Jacquet-Tisseau et annoté par Jacques Lafargue (Editions Allia: Paris, 2005); Margaret Atwood, "True North" in *Saturday Night*, Toronto, January 1987; Northrop Frye, "Haunted by Lack of Ghosts: Some Patterns in the Imagery of Canadian Poetry" in *The Canadian Imagination: Dimensions of a Literary Culture*, edited by David Staines (Harvard University Press: Boston,1978); Lewis Carroll, *Through the Looking-Glass* in *The Annotated Alice*, with an introduction and notes by Martin Gardner (Clarkson Potter: New York, 1960).

For the section on Ireland I found Cecil Woodham-Smith's *The Great Hunger: Ireland 1845–1849* (Hamish Hamilton, London, 1962) especially useful. William Trevor story "Attracta" appeared in *Lovers of Their Time* (The Bodley Head: London, Sydney & Toronto, 1978)

For the section on language I used Albertine Gaur, *A History of Writing* (The British Library: London, 1984), Wilhelm von Humboldt, "Uber das vergleichende Sprachstudium in Beziehung auf die verschiedenen Epochen der Sprachentwicklung" in *Gesamelte Werke in 7 Bände*, edited by Carl Brandes (Georg Reimer: Berlin, 1841-52) and Benjamin Lee Whorf, *Language, Thought, and Reality* (MIT Press: Cambridge, Mass., 1956) and, once again, Jean Bottéro's *Mésopotamie: L'écriture, la raison et les dieux* (Gallimard: Paris, 1987). Richard Dawkins's *The Selfish Gene*, Thirtieth Anniversary Edition (Oxford University Press: Oxford and New York, 2006) is, I believe, one of the few essential books of our time. I also consulted Peter J. Richardson and Robert Boyd's *Not By Genes Alone: How Culture Transformed Human Evolution* (Chicago University Press: Chicago and London, 2005). Nazim Muhanna's piece, "The Deafening Silence of Arab Intellectuals," appeared in *Asharq Al-Awsat* (London, January 15, 2007).

Other books I used are: Gertraud Gutzmann, "1940, Summer" in *A New History of German Literature*, edited by David E. Wellbery (Harvard University Press: Cambridge, Mass. & London, 2004); Ernst Pawel, *The Nightmare of Reason: A Life of Franz Kafka* (Farrar, Straus & Giroux: New York, 1984); Sam Hall, *The Fourth World: The Heritage of the Arctic and Its Destruction* (Alfred A. Knopf: New York, 1987); Robert Brightman, *Grateful Prey: Rock Cree Human-Animal Relationships* (University of California Press: Berkeley, 1993); Yves Bonnefoy, *Dictionnaire des mythologies et des religions des societés traditionnelles et du monde antique* (Flammarion: Paris, 1981); Michel Serres, *Le contrat naturel* (Flammarion: Paris, 1999); Roberto Calasso, *Le nozze di Cadmo e Armonia* (Adelphi: Milano, 1933); Claude Lévi-Strauss, *La pensée sauvage* (Plon: Paris, 1962).

4. The Books of Don Quixote

For the background on Cervantes's time and the question of the Sacromonte fakes, I read Manuel Rivero Rodríguez, *La España de Don Quijote: Un viaje al Siglo de Oro* (Alianza: Madrid, 2005); Contreras I. Pulido y R. Benítez, *Judíos y Moriscos herejes* (Random House/ Mondadori: Barcelona, 2005); Joseph Pérez, *Historia de una tragedia: la expulsión de los judíos de España*

(Editorial Crítica: Barcelona, 1993); and Manuel Barrios Aguilera & Mercedes García-Arenal (ed.), *Los plomos del Sacromonte:
Invención y tesoro* (Biblioteca de estudios moriscos, Universi-
dades de Valencia, Granada y Zaragoza: Valencia, 2006). Two
essays in this last volume are of prime importance: the quotation *"A María no tocó pecado primero"* appears in Manuel
Barrios Aguilera, "Pedro de Castro y los plomos del
Sacromonte." The first discoveries are analyzed in P. S. van
Koningsveld and G. A. Wiegers's contribution, "El pergamino
de la Torre Turpiana."

I used the Loeb Library edition of Virgil in two volumes,
with an English translation by H. Rushton Fairclough (Har-
vard University Press: Cambridge, Mass. and William
Heinemann Ltd: London, 1974) but quoted from C. Day
Lewis's version from *The Aeneid of Virgil* (Oxford University
Press: Oxford, 1952). My favourite edition of *Don Quixote*,
notwithstanding the excellent one published by Galaxia
Gutenberg and Círculo de Lectores (Madrid, 2006), is that of
Isaías Lerner: Miguel de Cervantes Saavedra, *El Ingenioso
Hidalgo Don Quixote de la Mancha*, Tomo I [1605], edición y
notas Celina S. de Cortazar e Isaías Lerner (Editorial Universi-
taria de Buenos Aires: Buenos Aires, 1969). Jorge Luis Borges's
"Pierre Menard, autor del *Quijote*" was collected in *Ficciones*
(Sur: Buenos Aires, 1944).

5. *The Screen of Hal*

Three cautionary books provoked several of the questions in
this chapter: Giorgio Agamben's *Stato di eccezione*; Jane
Jacobs's *Dark Age Ahead* (Random House Canada: Toronto,
2004) and Axel Honneth's *Verdinglichung: eine anerkennungsthe-
oretische Studie* (Suhrkamp Verlag: Frankfurt-am-Main, 2005).

The latter led me back to George Lukács's *History and Class-Consciousness*, [1923] translated by Rodney Livingstone (Merlin Press: London, 1971)

Jack London's words are taken from: Jack London, "What Life Means to Me" in *Revolution and Other Essays*, 1909, which I first read in French translation; Jack London and Arthur George, "To Be Abolished" in "Appeal to Reason, 30 March 1907," reprinted in *"Yours for the Revolution": The Appeal to Reason, 1895-1922* (University of Nebraska Press, Lincoln, 1990), edited by John Graham; and Jack London, *The Assassination Bureau, Ltd.* completed by Robert L. Fish, (McGraw-Hill Book Co.: New York, 1963). Stanley Kubrick's film is thoroughly examined in Stephanie Schwam (editor), *The Making of 2001: A Space Odyssey* (Modern Library: New York, 2000).

The quotations in this chapter are from: Constantin Cavafy, *Collected Poems*, translated by Edmund Keeley and Philip Sherrard, and edited by George Savidis (The Hogarth Press: London, 1984); Hebrews 13:8 in the King James Bible; Aristotle, *Politics* I:1:5 translated with an introduction by Thomas Alan Sinclair (Penguin Books: Harmondsworth, Middlesex, 1962) and *Nichomachean Ethics*, X:9:8-9, translated by J. A. K. Thomson (Penguin Books: London, etc., 2003); Julia Kristeva, *Etrangers à nous-mêmes* (Fayard: Paris, 1988); Aldous Huxley, *Brave New World* (The Albatross: Hamburg, Paris, Bologna, 1933); *Nunca Más: A Report by Argentina's National Commission on Disappeared People*, translated by Nick Caistor (Faber and Faber in association with Index on Censorship: London, 1986); Lauren Weisberger, *The Devil Wears Prada* (Doubleday: New York, 2003); George Eliot, "Silly Novels by Lady Novelists" [1856] in *Selected Critical Writings*, edited by Rosemary Ashton (Oxford University Press: Oxford and New York, 1992); David Foster Wallace, "E Pluribus Unum: Television

and U.S. Fiction" in *A Supposedly Fun Thing I'll Never Do Again*
(Little, Brown and Co.: New York, 1997); Victor Klemperer, *I
Will Bear Witness: A Diary of the Nazi Years, vol. I: 1933-1941*,
translated by Martin Chalmers (Random House: New
York,1998); Gamal Al-Banna, "Réflexions d'un religieux
libéral" [extracts from articles appeared in *Al-Raya* (Doha)
and *Al-Masri Al-Youm* (Cairo)] in *Courrier International* No.
848: Paris, February 1–7, 2007. Al-Banna is the great-uncle of
the controversial Islamic scholar Tariq Ramadan, and the
younger brother of the notorious Hassan Al-Banna, who was
killed by Egyptian government agents in 1948 after the murder of the Egyptian prime minister, and who founded in 1928
the Muslim Brotherhood, the extremist group whose purpose
was (and still is) to create a Muslim state based exclusively on
Koranic law. Cf. Malek Chebel, *Dictionnaire des symboles
musulmans: rites, mystique et civilisation* (Albin Michel: Paris,
1995). Gerald Manley Hopkins's poem, "The Wreck of the
Deutschland," is included in *Poems and Prose*, selected and
edited by W. H. Gardner (Penguin Books: Harmondsworth,
Middlesex, 1953).

INDEX